A Sort of Peace Corps

Wilfred Grenfell's Labrador Volunteers

Harry G. Toland

HERITAGE BOOKS
2019

HERITAGE BOOKS
AN IMPRINT OF HERITAGE BOOKS, INC.

Books, CDs, and more—Worldwide

For our listing of thousands of titles see our website
at
www.HeritageBooks.com

Published 2019 by
HERITAGE BOOKS, INC.
Publishing Division
5810 Ruatan Street
Berwyn Heights, Md. 20740

Copyright © 2001 Harry G. Toland

Index Copyright © 2001 Heritage Books, Inc.

Heritage Books by the author:
A Sort of Peace Corps: Wilfred Grenfell's Labrador Volunteers
Gentleman Trooper: How John C. Groome Shaped America's First State Police Force

Cover: The 1931 volunteers at Cartwright with Sir Wilfred Grenfell at right; Bevan Pumphrey (center) in boots; and Ted McNeill with suspenders. The Ford Model A truck was Labrador's only motor vehicle at the time.

All rights reserved. No part of this book may be reproduced or transmitted in any form or by any means, electronic or mechanical, including photocopying, recording or by any information storage and retrieval system without written permission from the author, except for the inclusion of brief quotations in a review.

International Standard Book Number
Paperbound: 978-0-7884-1758-0

For Sib and our children,
Weem, Deb, Phoe and Bob

Contents

	Preface	vii
1.	Prodigious Labors	1
2.	Grenfell	9
3.	A Sort of Peace Corps	27
4.	North, 1941	29
5.	Forsyth	41
6.	Cartwright	51
7.	From Pueblo to Park Avenue	67
8.	Sketches	77
9.	The Three Colleagues	99
10.	Back North	113
11.	Medicine Minus Mission	139
12.	Change	157
13.	Anne	173
14.	Hub	177
15.	Road	183
16.	The Grenfell	193
	Bibliography	199
	Index	201

Preface

The Grenfell Mission strove for more than eighty years to treat the sick and heal the injured of Labrador and northern Newfoundland, educate the coasts' children, care for orphans, and in other ways make possible a more abundant life. Founded by Dr. (later, Sir) Wilfred Thomason Grenfell, an English surgeon, it was primarily a medical mission but with a strong Christian bent.

Almost from the start in 1892 when Grenfell first came to the coast, volunteers joined in the effort. Over time the mission came to depend on them. Most were lay laborers, the rest medical people, both licensed and trainees. The great majority came from the United States, America's first big overseas volunteer movement, a sort of Peace Corps—private, of course, and different from the government program in important ways, but in spirit and purpose a sibling under the skin. For most of those who signed on, their work on the coast was memorable; for some, life-changing.

This book is about the mission and its volunteers—some famous in their later years, most of them not—what they did, what effect they had on people's lives and how the experience affected them.

It includes also sketches of Cartwright, a village a third the way up—or, as Labradorians would have it, down—the Labrador coast. That happened to be where I worked in the summer of 1941. It is also a kind of microcosm of Labrador's people, the ones Grenfell came to help, and a window onto how the mission worked and why a society outgrows a mission. I confess that I fell for the village and its people and its stories as it weathered changes piled on changes in recent years with the tsunami of the late 20th century rolling over the coast. Cartwright also happens to own the liveliest history of any community in that storied part of the world.

To try to digest all this, I went back to Newfoundland and Labrador in 1981 and 1991, forty and fifty years after the original trip, and finally again in 1999. I didn't plan the visits that way. My thought was to write this book after the first trip, but other events and projects in my life got in the way.

Scores of people helped, too many to acknowledge individually. I thank them all. Special gratitude is owed to: the three men who shared in our 1941 Cartwright experience, Arch Ruprecht, George Swift and the late Harry King; Bevan Pumphrey who passed on recollections and good will from England; Drs. Peter Roberts and Peter Sarsfield, generous in outlays of time and information; Gillian Hillyard, of the Grenfell Historical Society, who provided access to valuable documents; my son, Bob, whose help with the maps was inestimable; Amy Drinker who helped with the cover design; my wife, Sibby, Peter Binzen and Douglas Bedell, friends and former colleagues on *The Bulletin* in Philadelphia; Deborah Riley of Heritage Books; and Cecil Ashdown, of the Grenfell Association of America, who read the manuscript and offered cogent advice and assistance. They found errors that have been corrected, but I take full responsibility for any that remain.

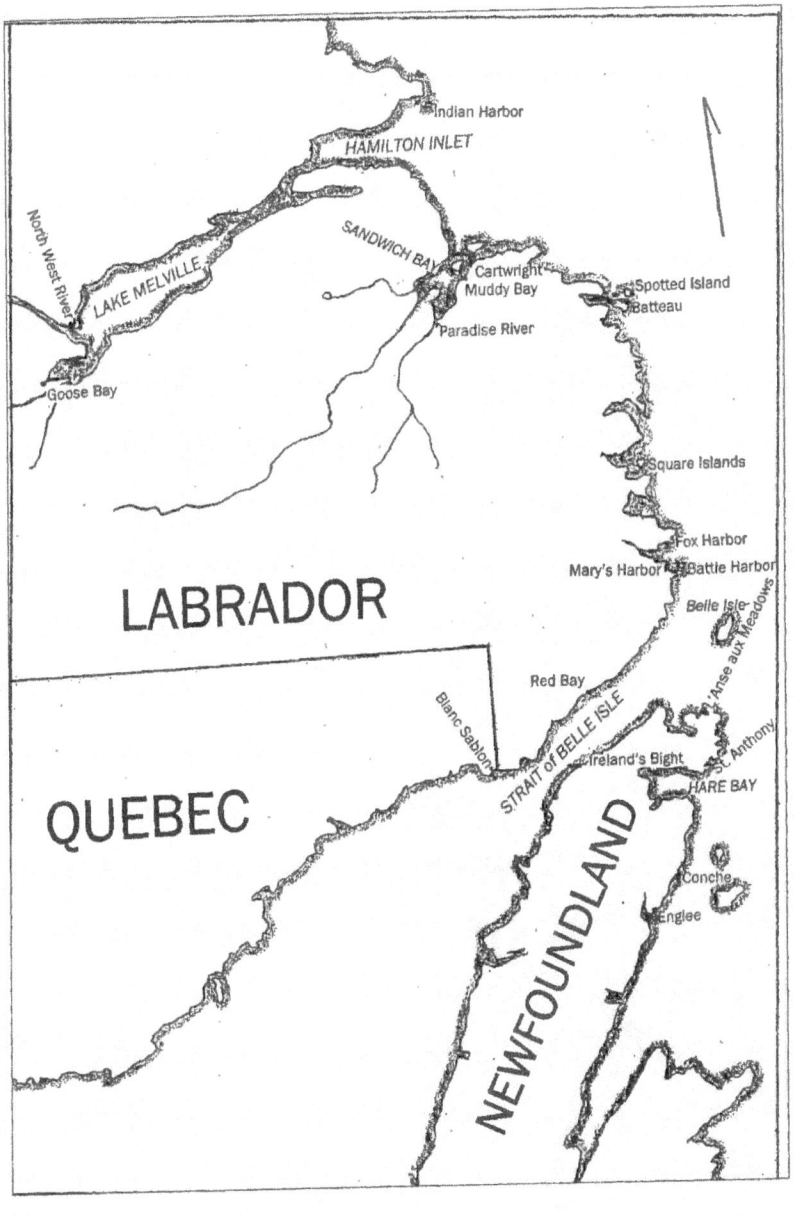

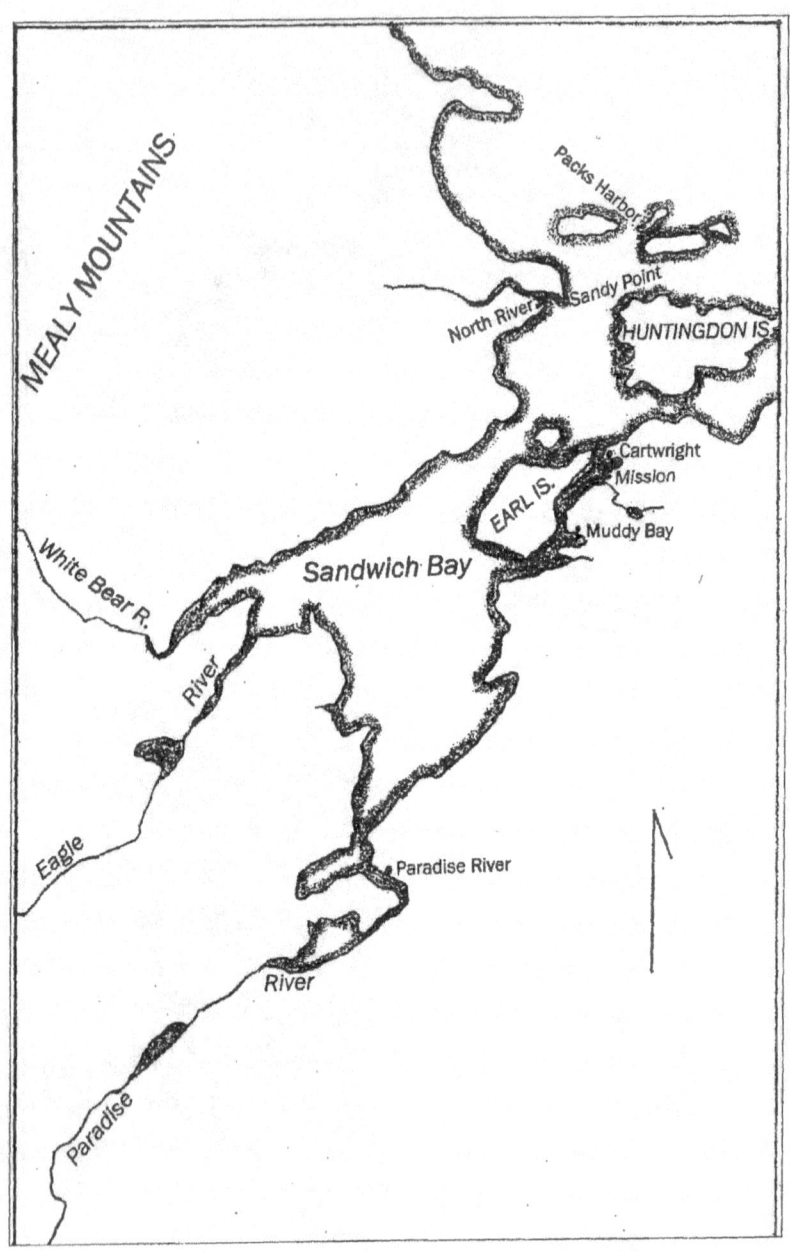

1 Prodigious Labors

The job—its key component, anyway—had the simplicity of a tide ditch for a child's sand castle on a beach. A trench four feet wide and six feet deep had to be dug from the Grenfell Mission station at Cartwright to a falls in Burdett's Brook almost exactly three-quarters of a mile back in the woods. Into the excavation would go a pipe to bring running water from the stream to the mission buildings.

Even today, with backhoes, bulldozers and heavy trucks, the project would be no small feat. But this was 1931 in Labrador. The available tools were hand saws and axes to fell the thick growth of black spruce and juniper trees, picks and shovels to hack through the tangle of roots and soil, two compressed-air jackhammers to break up the rock-like black clay beneath the forest floor, cordite as a last resort to dislodge otherwise immovable boulders, a Model-A Ford pickup to haul supplies from the wharf to the edge of the woods, a tiny 10-foot Cletrac tractor with a clanking caterpillar tread to drag materials up a primitive road that also had to be pushed through the forest, and wheelbarrows and two small gasoline-powered concrete mixers for construction of a dam at the falls that would create a pocket-sized reservoir.

The project's brute labor had to be sweated out amid clouds of voracious black flies, mosquitoes and other insects, against which the only defense was inadequate bug repellent. Rains sometimes fell for a solid fortnight and temperatures reached ninety-eight degrees in the sun. Labrador's winters can be savagely cold, but summer can make the sheltered woods almost subtropical. Wilfred Grenfell called it the toughest physical job his mission had ever faced.

The work force that summer consisted of sixteen mission employees—two from Cartwright and the rest from Grenfell headquarters at St. Anthony near the top of Newfoundland's northern peninsula—and fourteen WOPs. The acronym, we were told, without acknowledgment of its usage as an ethnic slur, stood for With Out Pay. They were the volunteer laborers of the operation. Supervising this disparate band of hard-knocks northerners and young students "from away" was Samuel Edgar "Ted" McNeill, the mission's burly, able construction chief at St. Anthony, identifiable by his suspender-hung trousers.

Grenfell, arriving on the coast in 1892, was acting on a report of desperate health care needs. He found conditions at least as wretched as the report had them, stayed and set up a diversified mission. By the time of his death in 1940, his colleagues were operating five hospitals, four nursing stations, two hospital ships, two boarding schools, a day school, an orphanage, a supply schooner and enterprises of homemade crafts, second-hand clothing distribution and agriculture projects to improve the diet.

Essential to the system as Grenfell organized it were the volunteers—the generally unskilled WOPs, along with nurses, medical students, dentists and doctors—who supplemented paid staff. Starting in 1894 with a helper named W. B. Wakefield who sailed from England to Newfoundland with Grenfell, legions of the unpaid were drawn north by the missionary doctor's charisma and pleas for help. Over eighty years, 3,500 of them served the mission. Almost all were young and nine out of ten came from the United States. Some of this crew, like Cyrus Vance, Nelson and Laurance Rockefeller, Francis Sayre, Clarence Birdseye and Henry Cabot Lodge, went on to later eminence.

Of all the assorted tasks that the WOPs performed or helped with none was more daunting than the Cartwright pipeline project. Late in his life, Grenfell said that when he stood on that work site, "I have literally taken off my hat because I felt I was upon holy ground." Another mission official quipped, "Unaware that it was impossible, we achieved it because we needed it."

Grenfell planned to make the Cartwright station his mission's "divisional" headquarters in Labrador. To do that, he was convinced, running water was required for its cottage hospital, boarding school and dormitory. The buildings, therefore, had to be located on the south shore of Cartwright's sheltered harbor, half a mile across water from the village's hundred and fifty residents on the north side. The choice made Cartwrighters' visits inconvenient but put the station within reach of the roaring torrent of Burdett's Brook, fed by lakes up in the hills. The year before, 1930, clearing of the pipeline path had begun. The grittiest work, however, remained for the 1931 contingent.

The first WOP on the scene was Bevan Pumphrey, a 6-foot, crew-cut 19-year-old graduate of Leighton Park School in Reading, England, and son of a North Yorkshire sugar refinery chief. Young Pumphrey, bursting with exuberance and zeal, had come up with the fourteen St. Anthony mission employees, including Ted McNeill, on the mission hospital ship *Maraval*. At its wheel was Dr. Harry Paddon, Grenfell's strong right arm at North West River, inland up the coast. They were joined by a couple of Cartwrighters, Charlie Bird, the mission foreman, and his son, Harvey.

Arriving not long after were thirteen American WOPs, mostly Harvard and Yale undergraduates, six of them from Massachusetts, two from Pennsylvania and the rest from various eastern states. One of the Pennsylvanians, Oliver W. Robbins, of the Philadelphia suburb Haverford, was spending his second consecutive summer at Cartwright. "A great crowd. They think no end of England and always respect anything English," Pumphrey enthused in his journal. His new colleagues elected him "boss WOP." They were lodged in the school dormitory, six to a room, and fed on cod, herring and salmon (a 25-pound salmon fresh out of the bay could be bought for a shilling, about a penny a pound).

Their initial eight-hour work day was exacting enough— "Sometimes at the end of the day I feel as tired as if I had played a hard game of rugger," the young Englishman observed. Soon, though, work hours were extended to 8 a.m. to 9.30 p.m. in Labrador's long summer days (Cartwright is on a latitude with Dublin). "Boss" Pumphrey found that "my most difficult task was to rouse them at dawn, in a variety of ways, from their well-earned slumber."

Early on, the volunteers unloaded supplies and gear, a task complicated by shallow water at the mission wharf which prevented berthing larger vessels. Thus, everything from 150-pound pipe sections to a cask of butter had to be handled twice, once from the supply ship to a dory and then from the small boat onto the wharf. "Unloading ten-hundredweight crates is quite a job when it is blowing hard," was Pumphrey's understated comment.

The six-foot depth of the trench was needed to insulate the pipe from Cartwright's 25-below-zero winters. But the fathom down was not easily won. "After the trees are cut down," the young diarist wrote, "the sod is cut with picks and hauled away. Then the soft earth is dug away and the roots hacked up. Below that there is black clay so hard that the picks can hardly shift it at all. And all the time we come across huge boulders that have to be blown up with cordite." He added later: "The labors we were required to perform were prodigious, especially when we fought the clinging clay in driving rain or were involved in an unrelenting struggle with shifting sand [in bogs]."

It was enough to inspire the Newfoundlanders to song:

I'm gonna stay where there ain't no clay,
Where there ain't no shovels and a half-day's pay,
Where there ain't no picks and rotten sticks,
And lots of flies with great big eyes;
Where there ain't no pipelines, oh so long,
To make you stop and sing this song.

Yes, lots of flies. George Cartwright, founder of the town, had warned in his journal that anyone going inland "will be incessantly tormented by millions of flies." They descended on Pumphrey and his crew: squadrons of Labrador's notorious diving, biting black flies, tiny sand bugs, blood-sucking mosquitoes, June bugs and hard-jawed deer flies, all of which "ruled with satanic ferocity," wrote the head WOP. "Every device known to us was used to repel this invading army, but Flit [and citronella oil] did not last, gloves were pierced, veils were only a devil's choice between black flies and suffocation. One eventually became so inoculated with painfully administered poison as to be almost immune from attack, but during the early stages, the sufferer is almost demented." Twice, bedeviled WOPs jumped fully clad into the iceberg-chilled harbor water to escape the bugs.

The aerial onslaught was so fierce that when the diggers paused for lunch there was no way to avoid ingesting the bugs that enveloped their sandwiches. The dietary additive ultimately triggered a brief mutiny by the Americans. Disgusted, they threw down their tools. Their leader, however, pushed a button that worked. "I said, 'All right, you can haul down the Stars and Stripes if you like, but I am going to keep the Union Jack flying.' That did it!" In a 1991 letter, Pumphrey looked back sixty years with generosity: "It was a momentary crisis which should not be allowed to tarnish the incredible loyalty of each and all of those boys throughout that summer."

After fifteen straight days of rain ("we are in oilskins wading about in water"), the sun broke through and with it came Grenfell—now Sir Wilfred—on the hospital ship *Strathcona*, accompanied by his son, Pascoe, working as chief engineer. Pumphrey, who had been interviewed by the missionary in England the year before, welcomed him on the wharf and was at his elbow on an inspection tour of pipeline work. Grenfell, much impressed, declared a holiday the following day and invited the volunteers to go with him on his ship to the mouth of the Eagle River twenty miles up Sandwich Bay.

The excursion began as a busman's holiday. The WOPs had to feed *Strathcona's* ravenous appetite for fuel by felling timber, rowing it to the ship and sawing it up on deck. After that came recreation. The Americans went up the river to fish, returning with a haul of twenty sea trout and salmon, including a couple of 8-pounders. Pumphrey accompanied the doctor on a butterfly hunting expedition, catch unknown. Half an hour with Grenfell, the young man wrote later, was enough for him to discover that "every act, every thought is in the service of his Master." On a brass plate around the ship's wheel he noted the inscription, "Jesus saith, 'Follow Me and I will make you fishers of men.'" Although the mission's founder had suffered a couple of serious heart attacks by that time, his young companion observed that "he could not be kept in a chair for more than a few minutes."

Building the dam at the brook's falls was the pipeline project's capstone. To collect sand for the concrete, Pumphrey and some of his colleagues were dispatched on shuttle runs on a 30-foot barge eight miles across Sandwich Bay to Sandy Point. There they shoveled sand from a 20-foot bank directly into the barge. On four of the heavily-laden return trips the barge went aground on The Flats in mid-bay and they had to wait for flood tide to float them free.

Dam work began with the diversion of Burdett's Brook into a new channel blasted from solid rock. Then a wooden form for the concrete was nailed in place. "Yesterday," Pumphrey wrote, itemizing a herculean volume of work, "we got through with thirty-four barrels of cement, 282 barrow loads of gravel and 141 barrow loads of sand. All this material has to be hauled through the woods from the wharf by the tractor. In another two days we will have the cement work finished. The concrete is being reinforced with stones, iron bars and wire." Before the concrete on the top of the spillway dried, the young Englishman cut into it the words "TM [Ted McNeill] HE DID IT—1931—WE WOPS HELPED."

At the end of the summer, after the Americans had sailed for home, Pumphrey was still there to greet Grenfell on a return visit. With McNeill and Charlie Bird, they walked the work site. A half-mile of the pipe, two-thirds of the total length, had been laid and covered. "As I walked along that long drain and thought of the spirit in which it had been made, honestly and soberly, I felt that the days of chivalry are not yet done," Grenfell wrote that fall to one of the American contingent, Thomas Lerch, of Wyomissing, Pennsylvania. "Of all the tough jobs on the Coast, that one at Cartwright has been the toughest... I hope with all my heart and soul, if you live to be one hundred, whenever you think of the Coast, it will give you a thrill to know you had a real hand in what appeared to be a difficult and thankless task."

Running water proved the blessing everyone had hoped for. The mere turn of a spigot handle brought the glorious luxury of a jet of clean water. A brief entry in the International Grenfell Association's 1932 annual report noted: "The water system has been finished now... No longer must we depend on the dog team to bring the water in iron casks from a brook a mile away." Ten years later, Cartwright's medical officer, Dr. Hogarth Forsyth, called the piped water "a great boon to the settlement as well as the station," even though it would be more than forty years before the mains would reach the village across the harbor.

Late in September of 1987, Pumphrey, graying but hale at 75 and retired from running the family sugar concern, returned for the first time to the scene of his youthful labors. By then, the 1931 water system had been replaced by a much grander one with a large reservoir farther up in the hills. With the help of powerful earth-moving equipment, the Province of Newfoundland had installed the new pipeline to serve the whole village as well as the clinic and its outbuildings, the only functioning remnants of the mission complex. The 1931 dam on Burdett's Brook, however, was still intact.

"Soon after I arrived at the clinic from [the coastal steamer] *Northern Ranger*," he wrote in a recent journal, "'Uncle Bill' had driven me along the road to the ravine of Burdett's Brook to point out a part of the dam shining white up there among the spruce trees. Now, like a mountain guide, he led me through that wild hillside until at last it was there before me, the flow of the river cascading over it and down the ravine below."

Through the clarity of the racing cold water the Englishman could still make out the letters he had scratched on the spillway fifty-six years earlier.

"As in a vision, I saw those splendid men as they labored in the heat, beset by flies, heard their laughter and shouting and the noise of the concrete mixers, the barrows and the tractor. They are gone now, with Charlie Bird, Harvey Bird, Jack Watts and Stewart Williams. The Labrador, for which each in his way gave so much, is the richer for them."

2 Grenfell

By the 1930s Wilfred Grenfell was a popular hero in England, Canada and the northeast quadrant of the United States, especially among middle-to-upper-class WASPs. He had earned his laurel wreath. Arriving at age 27 on the rock-bound coasts of northern Newfoundland and Labrador, he had found 4,000 fishermen and their families, "livyers," (live heres) whose forebears had emigrated from Devon, Dorset and Cornwall, Scotland and Ireland; 1,500 Inuit (Eskimo), and roving bands of Montagnais and Nascaupi Indians. Many of the coastal settlers were living in miserable squalor, suffering from tuberculosis, diphtheria, scurvy, rickets, beriberi, anemia and more. The scantiest Band-Aid of occasional health care was offered by a doctor on a coastal steamer during brief stops at ports of call. In that medical vacuum, the livyers treated their sick with charms and bizarre home remedies: haddock fins to ward off rheumatism, sugar in babies' eyes to cure ophthalmia.

The coast's 25,000 summer visitors—"floaters" fishing from schooners from the south or "stationers" living in summer fishing cabins with wives and children—also suffered all manner of untreated cuts, infections, fractures and illnesses. Many of them and the livyers were illiterate and in thrall to unscrupulous merchants under a notorious "truck" system: the fishermen handed over their catches in return for food and other necessities. All too often they were left in penury, debt and sometimes starvation.

One of Grenfell's early patients was a father who had watched three sons die of diphtheria. "I did not know what to do, doctor," the man told him, "so I greased the throat inside with a candle and tied a split herring around their throats." Standard treatment for wounds, he found, was to squirt tobacco juice on the cut and bind it tightly with a dirty rag. Inevitable infections followed. Yet nothing could be allowed to interfere with a man's work. The coast's iron reality was: work or starve, you and your family.

Grenfell came upon mothers so malnourished that they could not suckle their babies and had no money for the luxury of canned milk. "[They] had learned by experiment and necessity," he told a Philadelphia audience of physicians, "to predigest flour in their own mouths [and spit it into the infant's mouth] in order to carry a scrawny baby through until its salivary glands developed." He treated a small girl whose father had chopped off her feet with an ax. "They had become gangrenous in winter from frostbite through her wandering outdoors without shoes or stockings," he told a radio audience. The doctor set up distribution outlets where people could acquire donated garments for bartered items or some work for the mission. By the mid-1930s, the outlets were helping to clothe 15,000 people.

After he helped bury an isolated salmon fisherman and his wife near Indian Harbor on the Labrador coast, he was left with their five children sitting on the grave mound. "It wasn't a question of *wanting* to take them," the missionary said later. "By all the laws of humanity, we *had* to take care of them." Thus began the mission's orphanages.

In the three summer months of his first year on the coast, 1892, Grenfell treated nine hundred patients, cruising up and down the uncharted coasts of Labrador and northern Newfoundland on the 92-ton ketch *Albert*. The following year, he opened his first cottage hospital at Battle Harbor in Labrador. Across its two connected buildings in block letters ran the quotation, "INASMUCH AS YE HAVE DONE IT UNTO ONE OF THE LEAST OF THESE MY BRETHREN YE HAVE DONE IT UNTO ME." By 1902, Grenfell and his doctors and nurses were treating 2,774 patients, 110 of them resident in hospitals. Ten years later, the mission—it was never connected with a religious denomination—employed sixty doctors, nurses and teachers and carried an annual patient load of more than 20,000. And a decade after that, the organization was operating six hospitals, five nursing stations, two orphanage-boarding schools and a string of small summer schools on the coast.

Far ahead of his time, Grenfell knew that remedial medicine alone was not enough, that the whole person had to be helped. A tireless promoter of better diets and preventive medicine, he oversaw the planting of gardens and pasturing of two dairy herds on the coast. Endlessly, he urged people to eat the skins with their potatoes, to bake with whole-wheat flour. On his own motion, apart from the mission agenda, he dotted the region with co-op stores to offer lower-priced merchandise and allow people to escape generations-long debt to the merchants.

To augment the settlers' income, he promoted cottage industries for which they made tablemats, rugs, garments, walrus ivory carvings and toys to be sold in the mission's stores in distant cities. In 1901 he got a lumber mill going which was producing fishing schooners four years later. Soon after that he had a dry-dock built in St. Anthony at which 1,876 vessels were serviced over half a century beginning in 1928. "It may be objected," said a 1937 mission pamphlet, "that part of this work should be done by the government. In more thickly populated countries this might be the case. In north Newfoundland and Labrador the government has not been able to do it... the work would not have been done if Sir Wilfred had not started it and labored at it for 45 years."

In this explosion of energy and good works he conveyed a sense of virile, evangelical Christianity practiced by a man hugely enjoying himself. "Following Christ," he told an American audience, "has given me more fun and adventure than any other kind of life."

In his day he was as famed a missionary as Albert Schweitzer, equatorial Africa's legendary healer. (When they were photographed together in London, Grenfell's proposed caption for the picture, perhaps alluding to Schweitzer's girth, was "The African hippopotamus meets the Labrador polar bear.") A winner of the Nobel Peace Prize, Schweitzer was a man of more expansive intellect than Grenfell, a philosopher, theologian and musician. His repute fares far better today than the Labrador doctor's. Mention of Grenfell's name nowadays is likely to draw a blank stare from Americans under 50—from many over 50, too.

Yet *Time* gave his obituary in 1940 a full page. President Roosevelt, consumed as he was with war plans in 1942, paused to observe publicly the fiftieth anniversary of Grenfell's arrival on the coast. As early as 1912, Theodore Roosevelt wrote to him, "My dear doctor, you have done a very great work. I am so pleased that some of my countrymen have waked up and tried to help you in it."

They had indeed. By 1914, the first year the Grenfell organization kept such records, seventy manual laborers, teachers, nurses, medical students and doctors were serving in Newfoundland and Labrador. All but three were Americans and most were unpaid. It was a pioneering initiative in American volunteerism. Churches had sent missionaries abroad, most of them salaried, since early in the nineteenth century. The American Friends Service Committee organized thousands of volunteers to work in Mexico and elsewhere in Latin America, but that program didn't begin until 1939. The Grenfell Mission was the first beneficent institution to draw large numbers of American volunteers overseas.

At International Grenfell Association stores in New York, Boston, Philadelphia, Ottawa and London visitors could buy carved whalebone and walrus ivory figurines of Inuit hunters on skis, polar bears and seals; sealskin moccasins or hooded parkas made of "Grenfell Cloth," a tightly woven poplin of long-staple, waxed Egyptian cotton, still made in England. Besides providing income to the coastal people, the shops offered to potential volunteers tangible evidence of the Labrador's distant romance. By 1940, the IGA had fourteen branch associations in the United States, as far south as Washington and west to Chicago.

Sir Wilfred—King George V knighted him in 1927—spoke regularly as the association's fundraiser in cities and on campuses from Boston to the capital and even in California on occasion. He was not a polished platform speaker. His talks tended to stretch out and ramble. What held his audiences was his passionate commitment to his mission's work, his cheery, boyish sense of humor, his unabashed Christian faith and, most of all, first-person anecdotes about his sometimes perilous trips by dog sled and hospital ship along the bleak coasts.

He was not beyond milking a dramatic moment to advance the cause. A doctor colleague recalled that Grenfell, in New York to raise money, received word that a mission hospital ship had foundered and sunk in heavy seas, a grave loss. Three days later, speaking in Carnegie Hall, he arranged to be interrupted by a man walking on stage and handing him the telegram about the sinking. "Oh no! This is terrible!" the missionary groaned, as he read aloud the message. Pens were scratching on checks in the audience before he had finished.

Nor was he one to let opportunity pass ungrasped. In 1909 he was sailing in the Gulf of St. Lawrence on his hospital ship when the wireless operator came to his cabin. "Doctor," he told him, "I have intercepted a wireless message from Peary to Washington. He has found the Pole and is asking if he may present the mission with his superfluous supplies or whether he is to sell them to you." Grenfell's instant response: "Wireless Peary, 'Give it to them, of course,' and sign it 'Washington.'"

The doctor raised more than funds at his speaking engagements. He was after volunteers as well. A fisher of men, Grenfell trolled tirelessly for men—and women. "Come and help," he told audiences, and the thousands who responded ranged from specialists with large practices to teenagers practiced in nothing. For the young the lure was hard to resist: travel to a stimulating land of icebergs and northern lights and work in the magnetic missionary's inspiring movement. For some it became a rite of passage, a family tradition.

But at a price. WOPs not only earned nothing for a summer's work, they paid their way up and back—about $200 before World War II—plus a dollar a day for board, for a total of $250 or more. Especially in the Depression, that was serious money. No earnings on top of the expenses meant real sacrifice for a young person of moderate means. Some dug deep to go north. "They [WOPs] have come from every rank of society," Grenfell liked to say. The net effect of the system, however, was to attract most of the volunteers from families who could afford it. That posed no problem for the Grenfell organization: an affluent WOP household was a likelier source of later contributions.

A friend from school days, Archie Ruprecht, and I, along with two other WOPs, went to Cartwright, some two hundred miles up the Labrador coast, in 1941. We spent the summer at manual labor, though not on the epic scale of Pumphrey and his colleagues ten years earlier. We had heard about the Grenfell Mission at our respective colleges, and both of us had acquired some doodads at its store on Locust Street in downtown Philadelphia.

Our familiarity with the mission and its founder, however, probably grew more from the doctor's story, "Adrift on an Ice Pan," than anything else. The account originally was copyrighted by the Boston *Sunday Post* and then printed as a 15-page pamphlet with a green cover in 1908 by the Grenfell Association. But its status as legend took shape after publication of the story in a 57-page illustrated book the next year by Houghton Mifflin's Riverside Press. By 1923, 136,029 copies had been sold and another 42,742 by 1943—a total of 178,771—a sizable sale now, but huge at a time when the U.S. population was less than half of today's.

It was the kind of book an adult rejoiced in giving to a son or nephew for his birthday—heroic adventure with a happy ending. "The tale told in your little book is one of the most absorbing I have ever read," Admiral Richard E. Byrd wrote Grenfell. Related in the first person with Victorian digressions and later retold in his autobiography, the story still has currency in eastern Canada. In the United States it has been lost in the attic.

Grenfell had attended Easter services on April 21, 1908, in St. Anthony and was walking back to the hospital when he got word that men had arrived by dog team from Englee, some sixty miles to the south. They were urgently requesting that a doctor return with them. Two weeks earlier, the surgeon had operated on 15-year-old Charlie Hancock's femur, afflicted with osteomyelitis. He had left the wound open to be irrigated, but it had closed and now was infected. Amputation of the leg might be required, and quickly.

Normally, his driver, Reuben Simms, would have gone with him. But Grenfell wanted Simms to be able to enjoy Easter with his family. So he hitched his prized team of eight dogs to a komatik (sled) carrying medical supplies and his pet cocker spaniel, Jack, and set off immediately. The messengers and their slower team followed. They all spent the night at Lock's Cove, a hamlet eighteen miles west on the shore of Hare Bay. During the night the wind shifted to the northeast, bringing fog, rain and a rolling sea to the 40-mile, east-west bay. The next morning, the doctor sent his companions ahead. Two hours later, as more rain began to fall, he followed, planning to overtake them easily with his stronger team.

People at Lock's Cove had warned him against traveling on the Hare Bay ice in those conditions. For a time he skirted the shore. Then, impatient, he tried a shortcut across the head of the bay, filled with ice pans jammed in by the easterly wind. The ice to Hare Island, about a mile offshore, was solid enough, and he reached it safely.

Three miles beyond the island was the rocky rim of the bay's south shore, and he headed for it over the broken ice. He was only a quarter-mile from the land when the wind suddenly dropped, then swung around to offshore. At the same time he found himself in "sish" ice the consistency of porridge, a product of the grinding pans and rain, beneath the thin surface film.

The komatik's runners began to settle in the slob. Grenfell tore off his oilskins and yelled to his dogs to make a dash for the shore, but they sensed danger and hesitated. The komatik, with the doctor beside it, sank into the mushy ice and the dogs, struggling with the load, were pulled down, too. In that instant he recalled that James Hancock, father of the boy he was going to see, had drowned earlier in the year in just this kind of fix when he became entangled in his team's traces in slob ice. With his sheath knife he cut the komatik's sealskin lines to the team and wrapped the trace of one of his lead dogs, Brin, around his wrist. Brin managed to scramble onto a lump of packed snow about twenty-five yards away. Grenfell was pulling himself along the trace toward the snow island when somehow the husky slipped out of his harness.

It was perilous moment. His hip-length sealskin boots were filled with ice water; he had lost his cap, gloves, coat and overalls. The doctor was beginning to feel drowsy from the cold. Hope seemed to be slipping away when he noticed the trace of another dog nearby. He seized it and let the husky help him clamber onto the tiny snow raft. The success was momentary. The westerly wind was blowing them toward the open sea and it was clear to Grenfell that the packed snow beneath them soon would break up and they would be drowned.

"Twenty yards away," he wrote, "was a larger and firmer pan floating in the sish, and if we could reach it I felt that we might postpone for a time the death which seemed inescapable." After his first fall into the freezing water, he had tied his stag-handled hunting knife onto the back of a dog. With great relief he saw that it was still there. He grabbed the knife and cut the traces from the dogs' harnesses, splicing them into a long line which he divided at the end and attached to his two lead dogs. Then he pointed Brin at the larger pan and threw him off several times through the skim ice into the water. But the husky kept paddling back to the snow island.

Finally, he tried some strategy with Jack, the small black spaniel. He threw a chunk of ice to the larger ice pan and told him, "fetch." Jack, far lighter than the sled dogs, skittered across the surface ice and reached the pan. Now the lead dogs got the idea and made for the floe. Grenfell, hanging onto the spliced traces, took a running bellyflop across the thin ice, fell through, but struggled onto the 10-by-12-foot pan. Even that one was not enough to support them, so he immediately moved on to a larger ice island nearby.

His prospects were still desperate. The rising westerly wind was bitter cold. His clothes—a bizarre outfit of Oxford soccer shorts, red-yellow-and-black soccer stockings and a flannel shirt—were soaked with ice water. He cut off his boots at the ankle, opened the uppers and devised a makeshift windbreak for his back. He stripped and wrung the water out of his clothes. Into his sealskin moccasins he stuffed some unraveled rope from his dogs' harnesses, hoping to warm his ice-numbed feet.

Rescue, it appeared, was impossible: No boat could survive the pans he could see crashing in the surf a few miles away. The frigid wind was blowing him toward the ocean. He was teeth-chattering cold and night was coming on. "I saw that I must have the skins of some of some of my dogs... if I was to live the night out," he wrote.

Plunging his knife to their hearts, he killed three of the big sled dogs, Moody, Watch and Spy, stifling their death cries to prevent the other dogs from attacking the downed animal. "It felt like murder," he said later. He was bitten twice in the process. As he finished, he briefly pondered whether he might better turn the knife on himself if he did drift out to sea than "to die by inches." The dark thought was lost in urgent survival work. He skinned the dogs, fashioned a crude blanket from their hides which he wrapped around him, and piled up the carcasses as a wind-break. A matchbox he had chained to himself he found was soaked.

He stood up from time to time and waved but no response came from the rocky shore. As night fell, he made the largest dog, 92-pound Doc, lie down and, cuddling next to him for warmth, surprisingly was able to sleep. He awoke, shivering, in the middle of the night to discover that the wind had stopped. He went back to sleep.

It was still dark when he woke up again, convinced that he needed a flag on a pole to wave. His solution was to cut off the frozen legs of the dead dogs and lash them together with the sealskin traces to form a shaky flagpole. Though it cost him much in warmth, he tied his flannel shirt to its top as his flag. As the sun rose, he began waving this eccentric ensign at the shore, laughing out loud at the absurdity of wigwagging at the apparently empty cliffs.

Daylight brought some good news: with the air calm, the tide had floated him back up Hare Bay a bit so that he was now off Ireland's Bight, about five miles from the bay's mouth. He laid out his few remaining intact matches to dry in the sun and began looking for a piece of ice to use as a magnifier of the sun's rays. With it, he planned to ignite the matches and make a smoke signal by burning fat from the skinned dog carcasses. Running through his head, persistently and "quite unbidden," he wrote, were words of a hymn rarely sung in Newfoundland but recalled from boyhood:

My God, my Father, while I stray
Far from my home on life's dark way,
Oh, teach me from my heart to say,
Thy will be done.

No sign of life came from the shore even though he continued to wave his flag every few minutes. Meanwhile, the April sun started to thaw the dog legs, bringing unwanted flexibility to his "pole." The surviving huskies were gnawing at the remains of their teammates. At midday, he decided, he would kill another dog and drink its blood, "that is, if I survived the battle with him."

Peering toward shore, half snow-blinded—he had lost his "dark spectacles"—he thought he saw an oar flash in the morning sunlight. Impossible, he concluded. Between him and the coast were miles of heaving slob and pans which he doubted a boat could plow through, "though I knew that [if he had been spotted] the whole shore would then be trying." But it *was* a boat, and as it drew near some of the five men in it were waving and shouting for him to be calm and stay on the pan, not that he had much choice.

"As the man in the bow leaped from the boat onto my ice raft and grasped both my hands in his," Grenfell wrote, "not a word was uttered... though in spite of himself tears trickled down his cheeks." They gave him warm tea and some food, packed him and the remaining dogs and his flagpole into the boat and started back for Lock's Cove, ten miles away. The passage was rugged. The crew had to pry pans apart to make way and sometimes drag the boat over packed ice.

How did the rescue happen, Grenfell asked them. They told him two of the fishermen in the boat, Levi Reid and Levi Dawe, had been retrieving seal carcasses from a cache on a headland overlooking the bay the previous afternoon. One of them saw something alive on an ice pan as it drifted clear of Hare Island. They brought word to George Reid, Levi's father, who owned a telescope. He jumped up from dinner and ran to a cliff head with his glass. In the gathering dusk, he saw that the pan carried a man he believed was Grenfell, waving his arms.

Settlements along Hare Bay's northern shore were alerted that the marooned man was "t' doctor." Lookouts were posted on bluffs through the night. "The men told me," said Grenfell, "there were few dry eyes as they thought of the impossibility of saving me..." At dawn, through breakers swirling with ice pans that could have crushed their boat like an eggshell, the five fishermen rowed out to bring him back.

Grenfell survived with badly frostbitten hands and feet. Ted McNeill, who saw the doctor when he was carried back to St. Anthony on a sled, said his hands were the size of boxing gloves. Charlie Hancock was taken by boat to the hospital at St. Anthony a few days later. After an operation, he recovered fully. The doctor put up a bronze plaque in a hall of the hospital memorializing Moody, Watch and Spy "whose lives were given for mine on the ice."

The story is revealing of Grenfell: his phenomenal vigor, resourcefulness, courage, love of adventure and readiness to go the limit to help a patient. But his telling of it leaves a gap. While his dogs are mentioned by name a couple of times, nowhere does he give the names of the five fishermen heroes who laid their lives on the line to save his. The five—George Reid and his sons, William and Levi, and Levi Dawe and George Andrews, all of Lock's Cove—were praised anonymously by Grenfell as "five as brave hearts as ever beat." He later gave each a gold watch. But even ten years after the incident, when he recast the narrative for his autobiography, he did not identify them in print.

The British caste system of the era, perhaps. Grenfell was careful to name colleagues and significant contributors to his work, but rarely gave the names of ordinary people in his writings. It was not for want of rapport with these folks. He stayed at their homes, drank their tea, broke bread and traded jokes with them, and of course treated their ills. But recognition by name seemed to require special status, a little like being knighted.

Grenfell would probably be delighted to know that an annual Grenfell Ride—on snowmobiles—commemorating his ice pan adventure, was started in 1995 and thrives. For the year 2000 ride, 1,200 people manning 600 snowmobiles turned out. Their ride, of course, did not approach Grenfell's in adversity, but in temperatures around minus 6 F. and windchills twice that cold, it was no stroll on the beach, either.

The ride's sponsor, the Grenfell Historical Society, was calling it "the Northern Peninsula's biggest winter event." The ride takes most of the snowmobilers about fifty miles on trails from St. Anthony to Main Brook on Hare Bay, roughly following the missionary's track. Once in Main Brook, participants could get into a tug o' war, snowmobile races and competitions in log sawing, log throwing, nail driving, arm wrestling, lifting sacks of flour and, surprisingly, pillow fighting (a men's as well as women's event)—robust activities that no doubt would have appealed to the doctor.

Some missionaries have been remote, saintly figures. Not Grenfell. His dedication to the welfare of the sick and needy may have qualified him for a halo. (His stained-glass likeness, in fact, can be seen, garbed in boots and a hooded parka and holding snowshoes, in the "Physician's Window" of the Washington National Cathedral next to images of Christ the Healer and Dr. Louis Pasteur.) But he was too much of a sportsman, too joyful an appreciator of the ludicrous, too candid a commentator to allow for aloofness.

On the return trip to England from his first Labrador expedition, he was playing cricket on deck with the crew when their last ball went over the side. Without hesitation, Grenfell dove overboard, hollering to the helmsman to come about. It took two passes to pluck the water-treading doctor from the chilly North Atlantic, while the captain fumed. But the cricketer climbed aboard triumphantly holding the ball.

On the northern Labrador coast he organized sports contests among the Inuit and chortled as he gave the winners their prizes: scarlet army tunics and fox hunting jackets that had been donated to the mission. After a dinner on a wealthy visitor's boat, a fellow guest said that Grenfell "had us all in fits of laughter with one humorous story after another."

A morning ritual on his hospital ship called for the doctor and any WOPs he could induce to join him to plunge into the bone-chilling water before breakfast and race to the nearest ice pan. "It's great to be alive," he would shout, heaving himself onto the ice. The conditioning may have helped him survive his ice pan ordeal. Most Newfoundlanders thought the practice daft.

A friend, the Rev. Henry Gordon, the Anglican priest in Cartwright, was struck by Grenfell's "remarkable physical strength." He recalled a fishing expedition to Muddy Bay by him, the doctor and two "strapping American medical students" in two rowboats. On the return Grenfell, in his early 50s, with Gordon, 30, suggested a race over the three miles against a head tide and a "lumpy sea." The older men "won easily."

The surgeon's techniques were sometimes unorthodox. On the *Strathcona* he dropped in on the Newfoundland home of Captain Bob Bartlett, the rugged arctic skipper who had sailed with Peary. Bartlett's tonsils, Grenfell discovered, were swollen. He backed his patient against a wall, told him to open his mouth and inserted "something like one of those gadgets you used to snip candles," the sea captain recalled. "He kept snipping away until I could hold out no longer, so I pushed him away. I was sort of groggy... He was so interested, in his enthusiasm, that he did not realize he was doing this job without ether." Standing up, too.

Wilfred Grenfell would be labeled "born again" today. He was reared in the Church of England, but while a medical student at London Hospital he wandered into a tent revival meeting of the American evangelist, Dwight L. Moody, the Billy Graham of his time. Speaking that evening were the brothers, J.E. and C.T. Studd, English cricket stars, which piqued the interest of Grenfell, a player of rugby, cricket and water polo, an oarsman, sailor and hammer thrower. Rugged, he-man Christianity was being preached.

When one of the Studds asked members of the audience to stand up if they were ready to commit themselves to Christ, the apple-cheeked, mustached young medical student stayed put. "I was both ashamed and surprised," he wrote later, "to find that I was afraid to stand up. I did not know I was afraid of anything." Then a naval cadet near him rose and Grenfell, admiring his courage, found himself on his feet. He left the tent "feeling that I had crossed the Rubicon and must do something to prove it."

He joined the Royal National Mission to Deep Sea Fishermen as a waterborne missionary doctor, treating North Sea fishermen and bringing them Gospel messages in a direct conversational style. Within a year he was promoted to superintendent. In 1891 a member of the mission's council who was in Canada on business visited Newfoundland to look into appeals for help the council had received from the island. After inspections and talks with various Newfoundlanders and Labradorians, he wrote a 6,000-word broadside in the mission's periodical. It documented "scandalous" conditions of disease and poverty plaguing the fishermen and lack of concern in the colony. The report stirred an uproar in England, the most tangible result of which was the dispatch of Grenfell on the *Albert* to the coast the following year.

The doctor made no bones about the religious cast of his work. "I went to the Labrador," he told a New York audience, "principally to take to its people the teachings of Jesus Christ. I must frankly put the spiritual aim first and medicine second." The 1913 memorandum of association of the International Grenfell Association gave as its goal "the building up of and the extension of the Kingdom of Christ."

Oxford University, bestowing on Grenfell the first honorary medical degree in its 800-year history, declared, "... Up to the measure of human ability, he seems to follow, if it is right to say it of anyone, in the footsteps of Christ Himself as a truly Christian man." He regularly conducted prayer-and-hymn services on Sundays. His ship was never moved on the Sabbath. Mission buildings were bedecked with signs bearing scriptural quotations.

His "religious aim," while unwavering, was not tainted by sectarian prejudice, which he publicly disdained, along with racial bias. Mission facilities were open to everybody. The sponsoring committee he formed for the Grenfell Association of Great Britain and Ireland included England's Chief Rabbi, for which the doctor was criticized. "His doctrine is not any bar," Grenfell retorted. He welcomed Roman Catholics and Jews as employees and volunteers, and celebrated in print "a colored skilled civil engineer from Massachusetts Institute of Technology" who worked one summer on the coast. "My love for people early taught me that a different pigmentation of the skin from mine does not make my neighbor inferior," he said, a view hardly universal then. Or now.

The missionary practiced what he preached. Treating a half-starved Labrador timber cutter, he stepped out of the suit he was wearing and gave it to him. In his first winter at St. Anthony, he and a colleague were rebuilding a fisherman's hand, almost blown away by a shotgun blast. When fresh skin was needed for grafts to complete the operation, Grenfell donated some off his own body for the palm and the colleague gave his for the back of the hand.

The Labrador doctor—he called himself that though he never spent a winter there—had his stern side. He became a justice of the peace and set about implacably prosecuting traders selling illegal liquor to fishermen. (King Edward VII "laughed heartily," Grenfell reported, on being told that the new justice had signed on some American WOPs as special constables.) He could be irascible and autocratic. On one occasion, having found a man guilty of a brutal crime, Grenfell, like a latter-day Captain Bligh, had him roped to the mast and flogged. His administration of justice was not all grim, though. "We were permitted to make our sentences remedial... rather than retributive," he said, "and for lack of other entertainment our court trials were always exceedingly popular occasions." Lloyd's of London made him an agent and he hunted down and brought to justice at least one captain who had made a fraudulent insurance claim on the faked loss of a ship.

Such activities—in addition to the co-op stores he set up which competed with traders from the south—did not endear him to many establishment figures. Some of the press lambasted him. He was not beloved of St. John's merchants. His baleful accounts of conditions on the Coast angered some Newfoundlanders who accused him of running down the colony. Roman Catholic and Anglican bishops, alarmed by his nondenominational schools which threatened the system of government education grants per capita by denomination, opposed him. The Roman Catholic Archbishop of Newfoundland, stating that Labrador did not need "extraneous help," advised him to go home to England.

His defenders included those to whom he ministered. One veteran fisherman wrote to a St. John's newspaper, "There is not a fisherman I know nor a fishing skipper that sails a vessel to Labrador has anything but good to say of Grenfell and his work."

3 A Sort of Peace Corps

Grenfell's volunteer system had been going strong for more than fifty years when President Kennedy set up the Peace Corps in 1961. But it was not a model for the United States program, according to Sargent Shriver, its first director. "In our ignorance—my ignorance—we didn't know about the Grenfell Mission," said Shriver, a Maryland native, recently. "So we didn't talk about it as a model." It would have been surprising, however, if Kennedy, a product of Massachusetts and Harvard, hotbeds of Grenfell activity, had shared that ignorance.

The two movements had their similarities. In the early days, the Labrador and northern Newfoundland coasts surely would have qualified as a "developing nation," the Peace Corps's polite term for a Third World country. Deprivation was serious and needs pervasive, just like most of the 134 countries where Peace Corps people have served. Grenfell's greenhorns often did Peace Corps-type work, including teaching, construction and potable water projects, and shared a motivation to help people in need help themselves. And, as Paul Theroux once wrote of his Peace Corps experience, "we were the ones who were enriched," so it was for most of the WOPs. There were differences, of course.

The government enterprise calls for its members to receive three months of language and culture training, usually in the country where they will serve. Nine out of ten have college degrees and some skills. They are to serve a two-year hitch and live with a host family. They receive a monthly allowance, from $100 to several times that amount, depending on the country, for rent, food, travel and medical care. At the end of their 27-month tour they receive a "readjustment allowance" of about $6,000. Far from simple manual labor, they offer leadership in developing fisheries, forestry and agriculture and organizing health programs, vocational training and construction projects, as well as teaching.

By contrast, Grenfell volunteers received no training, were not required to have any skills (except for medical personnel), generally worked only during summers, lived in mission housing or on mission ships (except for teachers in remote settlements). Uncompensated, they paid their own way.

Until its latter years, however, when volunteer commitment began to flag and some local resentments sprang up, the system worked for more than seventy years as a model of volunteer overseas service.

4 North, 1941

We started for Labrador in mid-June 1941. The trip would bring us our first real-life awareness of the war. Daily, of course, everyone had been hearing about the fighting on radio and reading about it in newspapers and magazines. Now we would travel on a ship blacked out at night and in radio silence to avoid submarine attack. We would sail through a long convoy of destroyer-escorted ships bearing war supplies to England. By no means was it war up close, but it was the most immediate taste of it any of us volunteers had had.

In fact we were in something of a war zone. In 1941 German U-boats sank close to 300 merchant ships in the Atlantic, including ten under U.S. flag. Supplying allies was of crucial importance: three days before the year dawned Franklin Roosevelt had declared, "We must be the great arsenal of democracy." In March Congress passed the Lend-Lease Act opening the channel for war supplies to Britain and those standing with her.

In the pre-Pearl Harbor part of that year, though, America was still a nation at peace that could focus attention also on Ted Williams's .406 batting average, Joe DiMaggio's 56-game hitting streak and Whirlaway's Triple Crown victories. Hardly anyone noticed when NBC broadcast the first commercially sponsored television program to the nation's 4,500 set owners: a Philadelphia-Brooklyn baseball game from Ebbets Field on which the Bullova Watch Company paid $4 to give a time signal before the game.

Our trip north began in a Boston railroad station. Dr. Theodore Badger, a former WOP who had once stoked the boiler furnace on Grenfell's hospital ship, came down to see us off. Bound for Cartwright were four of us:

Arch Ruprecht, 19, a red-headed six-footer from the Philadelphia suburb, Wynnewood. He had been a year ahead of me at Episcopal Academy in Merion and now was entering junior year at Harvard.

Harry King, 20, of Jamaica Plain, Massachusetts, was a Ruprecht classmate at Cambridge, short, with thinning dark hair topping a bulldog face, bright, abrupt, opinionated. Only because it was wholly inappropriate, we came to call him the Bull Moose of the North Woods, Moose for short.

George Swift, 17, "Swifty," of Babylon, Long Island, was starting senior year at Pomfret, a Connecticut boarding school. He was the kid of our group and looked it—skinny, pale, teeth bound with braces and friendly as a puppy. Ships and their engines fascinated him.

I was 18 and headed into sophomore year at Yale, a lanky 6-foot-4 second son, more a farm boy than anything; I had worked summers on the family spread west of West Chester, Pennsylvania.

The sleeper train ride from Boston to North Sydney, Nova Scotia, was uneventful except for one discovery: an accompanying contingent of five WOPs bound for North West River, Labrador, included a girl, a blue-eyed, dark-haired charmer named Jackie Winslow. Mental wheels began turning. Why, we asked ourselves, were we headed for Cartwright when she was going someplace else?

North Sydney, a major port of debarkation for England, was teeming with Canadian and Newfoundland soldiers and sailors, some on farewell binges, many with girls. With hardly any layover, under a gray, wind-blown sky, we and a couple of hundred of the servicemen, got aboard the *S.S. Caribou*, a 2,222-ton Newfoundland Railway ferry, for the 8-hour, 100-mile ride across Cabot Strait to Port aux Basques on Newfoundland's southwestern tip.

The *Caribou* crew probably told us where life rafts and life jackets were stored. I don't recall; we paid scant attention. For us it was just a ferry ride, one more leg of the trip. Captain Benjamin Taverner was probably on the bridge that day.

A little more than a year later, in the predawn darkness of October 14, 1942, near the Port aux Basques end of the run, German submarine U-69 rifled a torpedo into the *Caribou*. Most of the 191 military and civilian passengers were asleep. Blasted awake, they scrambled groggily for life jackets, rafts and boats. The vessel, blown almost in two by the explosion, sank within five minutes. In the nightmare of confusion, only two of its six lifeboats were floated. U-69, which had launched its torpedo from the surface, dived to avoid depth charges laid down by the Royal Canadian Navy minesweeper *Grandmere*, the escort which had been patrolling to the rear of *Caribou*. The U-boat escaped undamaged.

One hundred and thirty-seven lives were lost, including a Canadian Navy seaman, his wife and their three children, fifteen other women and ten children, some of them babies. "If anything were needed to prove the hideousness of Nazi warfare," said Canadian Navy Minister Angus Macdonald, "surely this is it." Captain Taverner, 62, and his two sons, Stanley, 32, the first mate, and Harold, 22, the third mate, went down with the ship, along with twenty-eight other crew members, forty-nine Canadian service people, eight U.S. servicemen and forty-nine Canadian and American civilians. Among those lost was Canadian Navy nurse A. W. Wilke, the first of her country and profession to die in the war. Canadian naval crews saved 100 lives. At the time, the sinking was the worst marine disaster of the war in Canada's waters.

We reached Port aux Basques late in the day and boarded the Newfoundland Railway's narrow-gauge, all-coach train, the legendary *Newfie Bullet*. The two-day, three-night trip wound 640 miles at a stately pace around the island's perimeter. Up and down hills thick with spruce and balsam fir, across rivers and beside sun-splashed bays, the route often opened onto calendar-picture scenery.

Like the ferry, the train was jammed with servicemen, a few of them with girls, a number with bottles of strong waters. We slept in our seats. If one was lucky, there was room on the opposite seat to prop up a foot. The train poked along on its narrow-gauge tracks, stopping frequently at small villages. In these pauses, some of the soldiers and sailors would get off and chat up the local girls. From the turnouts, it was clear that the *Bullet*'s arrival was a high point of the week.

We ate in the dining car, each carload taking its turn. The process involved long waits to get into the diner and more waiting once at table. To bring meals to the hungry hordes, the train had only two waiters, harried to the edge of endurance. At our second dinner, we WOPs were sitting scattered among the servicemen. Ruprecht and I were talking and laughing about something when suddenly, across the table, a Canadian bosun's mate, his face crimson with rage and booze above a loosened collar, started yelling. As the rest of car fell silent, he wound up, glaring at me, "Any more out of you and I'll throw you right through that window."

A more mature traveler might have inquired about his grievance or as to how many helpers he might need to accomplish the throwing. I merely sat there, bewildered, shaken. No stranger had ever come on that strong to me for no apparent reason. What could have been said to ignite such a blast? The meal sank into subdued banalities. Afterward, Jackie, her blue eyes brimming with sincerity, congratulated me for "not getting sucked into an argument with that man." I didn't have the nerve to tell her my true state of mind. The seaman's indignation may have had nothing to do with what we said. Here we were foreigners—Americans often wrongly think of Canada as a sort of extension of the United States—civilians, at that, laughing it up while the Canadians and Newfoundlanders trudged off to a distant war. The anomaly wouldn't have taken much more than a few belts of Screech, the colony's notorious rum, to kindle outrage.

The next evening, our last diner dinner, we caught a murmur of the British Empire. Newfoundland at that point was very much an arm of what was left of the empire. The oldest British colony—first visited by John Cabot in 1497—it had been a self-governing dominion since 1855. But the island (with Labrador added in 1927), chronically poor, had been bankrupted by the Depression. In 1934 the United Kingdom took over its governance under an all-British commission which ruled until the colony became Canada's tenth province in 1949.

The three men who sat across the aisle from us may or may not have been members of that commission, but their accents identified them unmistakably as British, ruling class at that. We had been waiting as usual for about twenty minutes for the waiter—he wore badge #1 on his white jacket—to bring our meals. As he was passing between our tables, one of the men across the way raised his head and, in a voice of the Raj, boomed, "I say, Numbah One, what is the delay in the execution of owah awdah?" The waiter mumbled something about how many people he was trying to serve and disappeared into the galley. Not surprisingly, the first meals he carried back were our neighbors' across the aisle. In an American dining car crammed with U.S. servicemen, the tiny exercise in imperial privilege might have met with hoots and imitations. Here it didn't raise an eyebrow.

In St. John's, Newfoundland's capital at the easternmost tip of North America, we had barely time to glance at the old city, its frame buildings struggling up steep hills that sloped to a protected harbor, before boarding the *Kyle*.

The *S.S. Kyle*, hawsered to the dock, was not much to look at—a stubby, black-hulled, 230-foot spoon-bowed steel vessel with a derrick on its foredeck. But the ship was a tradition already flowering into folklore. Built in Scotland in 1913 for

Newfoundland-Labrador coastal service, the *Kyle* was girded with heavy plates to withstand ice. Two coal-fired boilers energized its three-cylinder, triple-expansion, 1,580-horsepower engine. Triple expansion, George Swift explained, meant three shots of power for one injection of steam.

The venerable workhorse hauled passengers and freight up and down the Newfoundland and Labrador coasts. For many little villages, with names like Fishing Ships Harbor and Indian Tickle, the *Kyle* was the only connection, physical and social, with the outside world. It was hardly a cruise ship, but at some ports the steamer took on the ambience of a country store, with gossip exchanged and stories told. Its arrival was big local news.

Richard Paddon grew up in Labrador's North West River, the son of Dr. Harry Paddon and his nurse wife, Mina. He recalled "celebrating the last mail steamer in October and the freeze-up because it was exciting with winter coming on, and with equal excitement the breakup of the ice in June. I remember getting stuck in the ice on the *Kyle* as late as July."

The ship is celebrated in a folk song, actually more a poetic recitation, "Smokeroom on the Kyle," which winds up:

> *Tall are the tales that fishermen tell when summer's work is done,*
> *Of fish they've caught, of birds they've shot, of crazy risks they've run.*
> *But never did a fisherman tell a tale so tall by half a mile*
> *As Grandpa Wolcott told that night in the smokeroom on the Kyle.*

The smokeroom, furnished with rows of benches, was indeed the ship's social center. Many of the passengers who got on to ride up the coast slept on the benches and ate out of blotchy paper bags. We WOPs lolled in comparative luxury, sleeping in small cabins on double-decker steel bunks and eating stews thick with cabbage and turnips in the dining salon. Arch and I shared our cabin with a laconic young man not much older than we, who spent most of the time stretched out on his bunk slowly nursing a bottle in a brown paper bag.

The *Kyle* slid out between the towering banks guarding the harbor's mouth and headed north. The routine at ports-of-call in northern Newfoundland and Labrador was to enter the harbor with a window-rattling whistle blast, drop anchor or heave to while one or two small boats put out from shore. A steward would let down the accommodation ladder for passengers departing or coming aboard. Gear and supplies would be lowered and raised by winch and boom or hand rope to and from the bobbing boats. The stairway would be hauled up. Then, with another deafening roar of the whistle, we'd be off again, skirting the moss-topped gray rock palisades. At night, we took care to keep the ship blacked out.

We were part way up the northern peninsula when the wider world intruded on our remote voyage. Late one day over a loudspeaker in the smokeroom came the familiar voice of Winston Churchill. Hitler, shredding a non-aggression pact, had just (on June 22) invaded the Soviet Union along a thousand-mile front and Churchill was commenting over shortwave B.B.C.

> "No one has been a more consistent opponent of communism than I have for the last twenty-five years," came the Churchillian growl. "I will unsay no word that I have spoken about it. But all this fades away before the spectacle which is now unfolding. The past, with its crimes, its follies and its tragedies flashes away. I see the Russian soldiers standing on the threshold of their native land, guarding the fields which their fathers have tilled from time immemorial..."

A pale afternoon sun slanted through the smokeroom's blue haze as the words rose and fell, sounding as though filtered through scattered clouds. Most of the small audience listened impassively.

> We have but one aim and one single, irrevocable purpose. We are resolved to destroy Hitler and every vestige of the Nazi (nahzzi, he pronounced it) regime. From this nothing will turn us—nothing. We will never parley, we will never negotiate with Hitler or any of his gang. We shall fight him by land, we shall fight him by sea, we shall fight him in the air, until, with God's help, we have rid the earth of his shadow and liberated its peoples from his yoke. Any man or state who fights on against Nazidom will have our aid. Any man or state who marches with Hitler is our foe...

Churchill at his most indomitable and galvanizing. Still, chilling questions arose again: How could Hitler be stopped? How were the subjugated peoples to be liberated from his yoke? If he throttled the Russians as he had so much of Europe, would there be any stopping him? How long could the United States sit on the sidelines and let others do the fighting? Churchill and his iron determination seemed the democracies' most potent weapon at that moment.

When we reached St. Anthony, near the top of Newfoundland's northern peninsula, we went ashore to be greeted by Grenfell headquarters people. Harry King made a pitch to be transferred to North West River, the so-called Eden of Labrador, more than a hundred miles down an inlet above Cartwright. He was turned down.

Back on the *Kyle*, we steered north again. Toward evening we entered the Strait of Belle Isle separating Newfoundland and Labrador, through which the Gulf of St. Lawrence opens onto the Atlantic. It was a principal corridor for convoys bound for England. Before us, stretching left and right as far as the eye could reach, were the blocky silhouettes of freighters with no lights showing in the gathering dusk.

Flanking them here and there were destroyers, angular as hatchets, knifing through the gray swells. We wove our way through the line of ships.

Past the convoy, dark on the horizon, lay Labrador, North America's right shoulder. The name, in those days at least, resonated with romance. Grenfell's headquarters may have been in northern Newfoundland, but he always referred to himself as a "Labrador doctor." A 1934 Grenfell book, in fact, was titled *The Romance of Labrador*. First seen through European eyes by Biarni Heriulfson of Norway in A.D. 986, the coast was named for an Azorean "lavrador" (landowner), Joao Fernandez, on an English expedition out of Bristol in 1501. He was the first on board to sight its shores. Jacques Cartier dismissed the coast's rocky fastness in 1534 as "the land God gave to Cain." On a land mass the size of Arizona, a 1945 census gave Labrador a population of 5,517, with a "stock" breakdown of 3,880 English, 699 Eskimo, 272 Indian, 265 Scottish, 166 French, 153 "half-breed," 57 Irish and 25 "other."

Shortly after the strait, we encountered our first field of floe ice, broken pans spread out like a bowl of snow-white corn flakes. We had seen growlers—small icebergs—which the *Kyle* had dodged. The floe ice had to be met bow-on, and the ship shouldered its way through the pans. When the crush was too thick for that, the rounded bow would be run up on the ice, letting some of the vessel's 1,050 tons crunch down to make a path. The ice scraped along the steel flanks as we passed, like a car brushing past an icy bush. It was cold enough on deck for topcoats.

At about that point, George Swift began to feel pain in his lower abdomen. We knew that he had been taking regular small doses of tincture of belladonna for what he called a nervous stomach. Our immediate conclusion was that he had overdosed on deadly nightshade, leaving him with a gut ache. A ship's steward gave him some Epsom salts. No doctor or nurse was aboard.

His condition rapidly deteriorated. He lay on his bunk moaning. His color went from pale to greenish. His eyes were glazed. Dried white spittle caked the corners of his mouth. We had never seen anyone that sick. He was close to dying, as we learned later, and that's how he looked. It was frightening, especially since no one on board really knew what ailed him or what to do about it. Ruprecht and I began reading aloud to him to take his mind off his troubles. One of us had brought along a copy of *Wuthering Heights*, probably the result of having seen the 1939 movie. We took turns at it—Heathcliff and Cathy on the moors over George's groans as we plowed north.

A bit farther up the coast, the *Kyle* got stuck in a fog-bound ice field. It wasn't for long, as it turned out. But the captain, increasingly worried about Swift's condition, broke radio silence with a plea for help. By lucky chance, a Grenfell Mission hospital ship was caught in the same crunch of pans about half a mile away, and its crew heard the message. Dr. John Crenshaw, a genial, curly-haired doctor hailing from Ninety-Six, South Carolina, picked his way across the ice jam to the *Kyle* and came aboard.

He examined George, gave him some sulfanilamide pills—the first of the "wonder drug" sulfonamides—and told him he had colic. "He knew what I had but he didn't want to tell me," Swift said years later. What he had was a ruptured appendix with peritonitis rapidly setting in, an often lethal condition. Crenshaw told the captain his real diagnosis and the compelling need for haste in delivering the invalid to Cartwright's cottage hospital, still a couple of days away. The sulfanilamide brought Swift a modicum of relief but he was still racked with pain. Someone, he recalled later, got him out of his bunk for Jackie Winslow's birthday party in the dining salon. He didn't have much to add to the festivities: "I was feeling awful."

The *Kyle* had dragged itself out of the ice field, but still had a schedule of port calls to make. Swift, unable to eat, was getting weaker. As the last day dawned before Cartwright arrival, the captain prepared to make a run for it even though we were wrapped in a blanket of fog that obscured icebergs known to be in the vicinity.

His stratagem was to post two men at the point of the bow and blow the whistle every ten seconds. If the whistle blast echoed off a berg, the bowmen would point in its direction, allowing the helmsman to change course and avoid a *Titanic*-like collision. Using this tense technique, we were running at three-quarters of the *Kyle's* 13.5-knot top speed. It worked. We thought it an exciting system, invented for the occasion. But it was old stuff on the coast. Grenfell himself had often navigated by echo. So, on one occasion at least, had a WOP. A malfunctioning appendix was the motivation then, too.

Nelson and Laurance Rockefeller, college students, had been working on the Grenfell hospital ship *Maraval* in the summer of 1929. They were headed down Newfoundland's west coast toward the end of the summer when Laurance had an appendicitis attack.

"We were hoping to avoid an operation up there," Laurance Rockefeller told me many years later. They urgently wanted to return to the family's summer home at Bar Harbor, Maine, before anything dire happened to the appendix. That meant catching the twice-a-week *Newfie Bullet* for Port aux Basques. But fog was holding them off the Bay of Islands. Nelson tried to coax the captain into sailing into the harbor through the soup, but the skipper balked. "Look, we know there is a cliff straight ahead of us and you can get a foghorn echo off the cliff so we will know when we get close to it," the future Vice President told him. "Then you can take a straight line, fog or no fog, into the harbor. This is an emergency."

The captain refused but surprisingly allowed Nelson, who promised to assume full responsibility, to take the wheel and give it a try. They inched ahead toward the cliff tooting the horn, turned in time, reached the harbor safely, caught the train and made it to Bar Harbor where the appendage was removed. "It took two incisions because the appendix was adhering to the abdominal wall," said Rockefeller, "so it's just as well we didn't have it out up there." Grenfell himself had offered to perform the operation, but "the young Rockefellers were having their doubts about putting Laurance in the hands of an ailing man functioning under rather primitive conditions as to antisepsis," a Nelson Rockefeller spokesman said.

The sun burned away the fog at mid-morning and the *Kyle* went up to full speed. The sea, we saw, was indeed dotted with icebergs—chalk-white, blue-streaked lumps shaped like sand castles, with tunnels and bridges and turrets, their contours softened by melting on the slow drift down from Greenland and Baffin Island.

In bright sun now, we churned through the windy passage west from Grady Harbor, through the strait below Huntingdon Island, turned sharply to port after entering Favorite Tickle and dropped anchor in Cartwright harbor. Several open boats came out to meet us, a couple each from the northern, village shore and from the mission on the south side. In the first mission boat stood Dr. Hogarth Forsyth, the station's medical officer, a short, wiry, sharp-eyed bantam of an Englishman, his thinning dark hair covered by a navy blue beret.

Two men carried George Swift down the gangway on a stretcher. Semiconscious, his complexion still the color of broccoli soup, he waved feebly to us, reflexively friendly.

5 Forsyth

C. Hogarth Forsyth, whom we came to know quite well, was one of the mission's unsung. He was as much a missionary doctor—and a competent one—as Grenfell or Harry Paddon. But outside of the mission's world and Labrador he was virtually unknown, like the Ecclesiasticus worthies "who have no memorial." He came to the Grenfell Mission from Westcliff-on-Sea, Essex, east of London, in 1931 as a staff physician and surgeon on the *Strathcona*. He ended up serving at more stations than any other IGA physician. After practice on the hospital ship and at Harrington, St. Anthony and Mary's Harbor stations, he was sent up the coast to Cartwright in 1938, three years before our summer there. With him went Clayre Ruland Forsyth, an auburn-haired, cigarette-puffing nurse from Augusta, Georgia, whom he had married when they were both posted at Mary's Harbor. They were childless.

In a "Dear Sir Wilf" letter to Grenfell in August, 1938, he described his arrival in Cartwright on his own "seaworthy little cabin cruiser" *Unity* as "one of the great moments of my life." He knew that he was to be the first medical officer stationed there, the mission's hub on the Labrador coast. He pledged in the letter to put "myself heart and soul into that." Forsyth found Cartwright's Lady Maclay Hospital, named for the wife of a Scottish donor, to be "the nicest small hospital I have ever worked in."

He threw himself into the work. In the hospital, with beds for eighteen adults and two children, a summer's in-patient load could reach one hundred, out-patients 1,500. Yet on a year-round average, medical work took about four hours of his day, he said, the rest going to station administration. Summers, treating patients on the hospital ship *Maraval*, the doctor cruised as far north as Nain, two-thirds the way up the coast, and to Seal Islands Harbor, eighty miles southeast. His annual winter dog-sled trip covered almost a thousand miles of much the same territory.

The lean little doctor had an ambivalent view of Labrador culture. "A psychologist," he wrote in a 1940 issue of England's *Medical Press and Circular*, "would find Labrador of inexhaustible interest. The nearest parallel is to be found in Rose Macaulay's 'Orphan Island.' Here are a people, largely of Anglo-Saxon descent, who have been isolated very completely in family groups for the best part of a century." Physically, they are small, he added, men averaging about 5-foot-5, "probably due to generations of dietary deficiency, though it is possible that in-breeding may have something to with it." Their diet was high in carbohydrates, meat and fish, with "vegetables and fruits until very recently very rare." Beriberi was not uncommon, "chiefly among the submerged tenth who are always on a bare subsistence ration of bread and tea. It is noticeable that the incidence of beriberi drops considerably when brown flour is substituted for white." Resistance to sickness, especially tuberculosis, was low, yet "both men and women are possessed of great physical strength."

A third of the population, he wrote, "man, wife and anything up to ten children and any other dependents such as aged parents live, eat and sleep in a one-room shack, about twelve by fourteen feet, permanently heated to about eighty degrees by a roaring wood stove. Another third lives in well-built, two-story frame houses... mostly in the neighborhood of the half-dozen larger bays." Since home-sawed lumber was readily available and everyone built his own house, "there is no need to point the moral to adorn this tale," he added. He gave no accounting of the final third.

> *All refuse, liquid and solid, is thrown out not more than ten feet from the door. The dogs cheerfully eat all the solid refuse, nature taking care of her own. Few people are interested in conveniences. The woods are literally all they need, spruce shoots good, if rough,*

toilet paper, and the dogs replace the sewage works. For some obscure reason, human excrement is their choicest luxury, a banquet worth fighting for.

The doctor, a no-nonsense, proper Englishman, helped run the dormitory of the station's Lockwood School, named after a Texan benefactor. The school was home to thirty to fifty children from up and down the coast during its 9-month school year. "They have highly individualized personalities and are very attractive, but----," he wrote of the students. "There is no great difficulty in teaching them the Three Rs, but when it comes to the point of trying to instill into them the rudiments of morality, in its widest application, the fun begins. They have none of those fundamental ideals on which teachers build and to which they can appeal in the ordinary child. Ambition? They have none. Discontent? They (and their parents) are a great deal happier in their primitive existence than we are in our more sophisticated one."

"Sexual taboos?" he continued, "Completely unknown. These children are acquainted with the 'facts of life' from the cradle up, and a perfectly free sexual inter-relationship begins at about the age of sixteen. Naturally, it is completely undiscouraged by the parents; it continues indefinitely until old age, and marriage is only an incident by the wayside. The uneducated parents set little store by education, and the main inducement to send children to boarding school is to get them fed and clothed during the winter."

These were broad strokes with a large brush. Some Labradorians made substantial sacrifices to send relatives to Lockwood for learning experiences that often led on to better things. On sexual relationships, Dick Paddon recalled his North West River youth: "The Church of England got around only once in three years. By then you might have one or two kids. It was not frowned on. But after marriage, that was something else... Children were an economic necessity. The more you had, the richer you were. Life took manpower. I remember Malcolm McLean—white beard, black hat, black coat that came to his knees, lived at Kenemish twelve miles away. He sired twenty-three kids, two by his first wife, twenty-one by his second. He went on to be one of Labrador's leading citizens."

Forsyth grappled with the missionary's perennial problem: "This introduces the argument that here is a perfect example of the modern idea of a completely uninhibited, natural childhood. Perhaps it is all right; why cannot the missionary leave it alone? Why *must* they try to introduce an alien morality?" The "plain answer," he added, was that "any study of the social history of the Coast through the last few generations shows undoubted physical deterioration following in the train of steadily increasing moral latitude. Cause and effect." If such a study existed, however, he did not cite it.

But he also counted redeeming strengths in the people. "The Eighth Commandment [against stealing] is seldom transgressed, the Sixth [against murder] never, and everyone will share his last crust with his neighbor or a chance traveler... There is no denying the fact that most people are very well adapted to their environment and lead happy, carefree lives. They are very clannish and have a wholesome contempt for anyone who is not a Labradorman, based on the inability of most outsiders to perform a fraction of the tasks at which they are so proficient." Capping this mixed view of his neighbors, he wrote, "They are a difficult people to work among, and those who have claimed otherwise have usually done so from ignorance rather than knowledge. Nonetheless, because they are the world's super-realists, we do thoroughly enjoy working among them."

Like most Labrador doctors, he made house calls unheard of for temperate-region practitioners.

"Once, on a routine trip," he told his English colleagues, "I visited a tiny shack and found there lying on the floor a young girl with a 24-hour-old bullet wound of her head. I cleaned up the wound, we dumped some of our gear, fixed her up a bed on the komatik and set out on the 80-mile journey to the nearest hospital. This proved no overnight job but two and half of the longest days I ever knew, alternating between walking ahead of the dogs on snowshoes to break trail and squatting behind the girl's head, holding it cupped in one's hands to break the pain of the bumps. Komatiks have no springs and make rough ambulances at the best. With the accustomed hardihood of her race, she stood the journey well, and lived to get married and have children."

Then there was the occasion, during the "in-between time" of autumn, too late for boats and too early for sleds, when he was walking back from seeing a patient and arrived at a hamlet for the night to find a boy down with acute appendicitis. "I had not the equipment with me for an appendectomy, and it became imperative to get the boy to hospital. I told the father this was the boy's only hope. He made a wry face and went out to discuss it with the other men. They agreed that if this was the only chance of saving his life, they would make it somehow. With daylight the next morning I saw the problem they were up against. The settlement was at the bottom of a mile-long arm of the sea. It was frozen over with young ice which would not bear, but through which no boat could proceed. The shores were lined by dense woods right down to the water's edge."

"The men made a box," his account continues, "put mattress and bedding in it, and the boy. Then four men each took one end of two long poles rigged sedan-chair-wise. Sixteen more men went ahead with axes and cleared a mile-long path through the woods around the shore out to the edge of the ice. Luckily, at this point a motor boat had recently been hauled out off the water, and she was speedily relaunched. But this was not the end of the difficulties. A mass of slob ice had drifted in and pinned the boat to the shore. It took all the men on a long rope to haul the boat out clear of this. Then we had ten miles of open sea to cover, with spray flying in and freezing solid as it fell. However, the boy was none the worse for it, duly arrived at the hospital, was operated on and recovered." If the story illustrates the rigors of Labrador medical practice, it hardly documents the "physical deterioration" of Labradorians.

Forsyth confided to Grenfell in another letter that "the dream of my life" was to own a boat and be its skipper and own a dog team and be its driver. In Cartwright he had realized both halves of the dream, although two of his teams had to be destroyed because of attacks on children. Yet he seems to have derived a deeper satisfaction from his association with the Lockwood School students.

"Children [at Lockwood] are drawn from extremely isolated tiny communities," he wrote in the Grenfell Association's journal, *Among the Deep Sea Fishers*, "and the experience of the last few years has shown that they react more to familial rather than the larger and institutional kind of life." Clayre had quit nursing and, in addition to keeping house for her husband, was the school's dormitory superintendent. Perhaps compensating for lack of their own children, the doctor and his wife became house-father and -mother to the pupils. "The relationship," he said, "is very literally carried out."

They ate two meals a day with the children, he at the head of the boys' table, she at the girls', encouraging them to discuss world events. They taught their young charges English folk dancing. "Saturday evenings are keenly looked forward to," he wrote, "when all forgather in the dining room for dancing and games while a log fire glows on the open hearth." They involved almost every student in staging musical plays, one at Christmas, the other at Easter. The doctor and some of the boys split firewood together before breakfast; at recess, he played spirited soccer with them. In May they observed Sports Day which included tug-o'-war, high jump and boys' and girls' 100-yard dashes, with a pistol shot by the village's Mountie to start the race. Sunday evenings, Forsyth conducted Evensong in the dining room. "I am mighty proud of our little school," the medical officer wrote to Katie Spalding, the Grenfell Mission secretary in London in 1943. "Clayre and I have had a free hand with it the last two years and have put everything we know into it."

Most of the children did not have to be dragooned into attending the Grenfell school at Cartwright, even though it meant long stays away from home. Forsyth told of their response during a medical visit he made to Seal Islands Harbor in the fall of 1942. A cluster of kids met him at the dock and followed him from house to house as he made his rounds in the settlement, even when it grew dark. "They did not mean to miss their chance of getting booked for school," he wrote.

Charlotte Bird, now of Cartwright, was nine years old when she went to Lockwood School for three years in the early 1960s. The Forsyths were gone from Cartwright by then. Charlotte came from Batteau, a tiny fishing hamlet sixty miles down the coast which had a school but couldn't recruit teachers for it. The Lockwood school year was more than nine months straight through. The sole opportunity to communicate with their families came a couple of days before Christmas when they were given time just to say hello and Merry Christmas over the mission radio-transmitter. "You couldn't really talk," she said. "Everybody was crying anyway. People would get very lonesome for home and parents, but if we wanted an education, that was the only way to get it." Teachers were "very strict... they made us study. Saturday was scrubbing day for boys and girls. We had to scrub down the whole dorm. Every Sunday morning everybody had to walk across the [harbor] ice to church, and Sunday evenings there was a service in the dorm for us." There was plenty to eat and drink, she recalled, parties at Christmas and Hallowe'en and an egg hunt at Easter. In a ritual that mystified them, the children had to give up their own clothes for the school year when they arrived at school and wear second-hand donated garments, some of which were "patches on patches," she said.

Chesley Lethbridge, who came to Lockwood School at age eleven in the early 1940s from his home at Paradise River at the head of Sandwich Bay, spoke of the doctor and his wife forty years later. "They taught you how to look after yourself," he said. "The Forsyths were very fine people. They were a mother and father to me and all the children there."

As the bombings of London intensified, Forsyth received direct bulletins from Katie Spalding, who lived as well as worked in the city. In August, 1940, she wrote him: "We are having it pretty hot in London right now, day and night attacks. Last night the attack lasted ten hours and as each night darkness falls earlier, I suppose we must be prepared for even longer raids. The gunfire and falling bombs do not tend to peaceful rest." A few months later: "My home district has been badly hit with five land mines, the most destructive of all. Several members of my family had a marvellous escape... We have to realize that any night our houses may fall in ruins and we with it... The noise of gunfire is terrific."

These vivid tableaux, along with the news that his brother had been taken prisoner by the Germans, raised an urgent debate in the doctor's mind. Up to that point, he had felt an unequivocal call to serve in Labrador. But now his homeland tugged. Should he return and offer his medical expertise to one of the armed services or to beleaguered Londoners? Where was he needed most? He wrote to Spalding, "My departure is going to create an impossible situation for Cartwright at this point. The thing to be decided is: Is a little thing like 'chaos in Cartwright' to weigh against the other? But equally... am I so vitally indispensable to my country, either?" He asked her to confer with IGA officials. She cabled him back: "Doctors not urgently needed. Now impossible to foretell future. [Denley] Clark and other doctors feel you should remain unless adequately replaced. [Sir Henry] Richards [a Grenfell confidant] feels American substitute desirable but decision rests with you... Need here indefinite. Strongly advise stay special work in Labrador." In a follow-up letter, she told him, "I had a cable from Dr. [Charles] Curtis [Grenfell's successor as superintendent on the Coast] saying how essential it was you should remain in Labrador, and neither Denley nor I know who could adequately replace you at such short notice."

Ultimately, he decided to stay on in Cartwright, returned to England in the 1950s and died there. Dr. Robert B. Salter, a Canadian Grenfell medical volunteer and later IGA board member, knew Forsyth in St. Anthony. "He was a capable person," Salter said. "I liked him. He led a lonely life. He was the only doctor for miles around." Dr. Gordon W. Thomas, whose Grenfell service began in 1946 and was IGA executive director from 1962 to 1979, knew Forsyth and called him "a capable doctor. He was dominated by his wife. He did a lot of work under difficult circumstances. People of Cartwright thought a lot of him. I felt sorry for him. He was a somewhat lonely figure."

6 Cartwright

George Cartwright, born in Nottinghamshire, England, was thirty years old when he came upon Sandwich Bay in 1775. The bay, 230 miles up the 700-mile Labrador coastline and fed by three surging rivers, he named after a kinsman, John Montagu, the fourth Earl of Sandwich and eponym of the bread-bound edible. Cartwright, later an army major, was described by contemporaries as a handsome man of "herculean frame." He gave his own name to the settlement he established in a shielded harbor at the bay's mouth. "The face of nature was so greatly and suddenly changed, as if we had shot within the tropics," he hyperbolized in his journal about his entry into the harbor. He built himself a house at the west end of its north shore and called it Caribou Castle.

His aim was to trade and promote "friendly intercourse with the savage Eskimaux," to trap and hunt for furs and to fish. Shortly before he reached the coast a band of traders had raided the encampment of a local tribe, shot some of them and had stolen their entire stock of fish and fur. Cartwright, entirely unafraid, arrived and went ashore with only his old army swagger stick and few samples of his wares.

"Then an extraordinary thing happened," wrote the Rev. Gordon referring to Cartwright's journal. "A young lad grabbed hold of a string of beads and was making off with it when Cartwright seized him, laid him across his knee and soundly spanked him. It happened that the boy was the chief's son, and whether it was Cartwright's cool courage or because the chief was not averse to his son getting what he deserved, the result was a complete change in the tense atmosphere.

"The chief took Cartwright's hand and then and there entered into a solemn pact of peace and good will. For years after this Cartwright carried on a regular trade with the people of the coast, deepening the feelings of friendship and affection and building up a very profitable business."

He and about a dozen men he had brought with him from Devon and Cornwall—the contingent grew later—along with his housekeeper and mistress, a Mrs. Selby, found an overflowing cornucopia of wildlife. In one three-week period, the settlers took 12,396 salmon from Sandwich Bay's rivers.

During the salmon run, he reported in his copious journal, "In White Bear River you could not fire a bullet into the stream without killing one." At one time, on that river's banks he counted thirty-two polar bears pawing salmon from the current. He shot six of the bears in one day but could collect only one skin. "It was the noblest day's sport I ever saw," he wrote.

Seals were abundant in the bay. He ran down foxes with his greyhounds and snared caribou with nooses slung under trees. On one occasion the men broke out in rashes, brought on, Cartwright theorized, by consuming five pounds of venison per day per person. The profusion of fish and game must have been enough to slake even his ravenous appetite; in England he routinely devoured an entire leg of mutton at a sitting. To supplement their surfeit of protein he planted Cartwright's first vegetable gardens, probably the first on the whole coast. Fertilized with ashes and rotting seaweed, over the years they yielded French beans, Indian corn, barley, oats, wheat, radishes, peas, cucumbers, turnips, cabbages, spinach, cauliflower and even asparagus.

He spent sixteen years "down on the Labrador," five of them at Cape St. Charles, lower on the coast, before settling at Cartwright. During that time he won the trust and friendship of the area's Inuit and Montagnais Indians despite some outrageous bartering. "One afternoon," he boasted in his journal, "I got three cwt. [hundredweight of] whalebone, one wolf and one black bear skin, ten seal skins, nineteen fox skins, twelve deer, four otter, two marten (sables) for a few beads and trifles of no commercial value."

Paterfamilias Cartwright performed marriage ceremonies for his men and native women, midwifed the births of their children (in or out of wedlock), doled out medications and administered bleedings, rationed allotments of rum, conducted prayer services, enforced discipline with beatings and buried the dead—the bodies sewn in canvas bags and dispatched through holes in the ice in wintertime.

He took five Inuit back to England for a visit that included an opera performance, riding to hounds and sightseeing in London. They were not impressed. One of them, Attuiock, commented, "Here are too many houses, too much smoke, too many people. Labrador is very good. Seals are plentiful there. I wish I was back again." The wish went tragically unfulfilled: Attuiock and three of the others died of smallpox in England; the fifth, Caubvick, a woman, survived the disease. Yet, back in Cartwright, their kin and neighbors heaped no blame for the deaths on the major and were as friendly and solicitous as ever. He borrowed an Inuit's wife, along with their children, for one seven-months-long winter.

Late in the Sandwich Bay years, Mrs. Selby gave birth to a child, but refused to swear that Cartwright was the father. His servants accused her of sleeping with Joseph Daubeny, the chief's assistant, who later confessed. Cartwright thereupon formally "divorced" her and stripped Daubeny of authority. All three returned to England on the same ship. It is a rare divorce that ends as amicably as theirs: Cartwright conveyed Mrs. Selby by four-in-hand coach to her brother's home and settled upon her an annual allowance.

The major was finally done in by assorted losses and a raid by the Boston privateer John Grimes who robbed him of almost everything. He and most of his band returned to England in 1786 (a shipmate on the voyage was Benedict Arnold). The frontiersman held onto his interest in the trading post at Cartwright until Hunt & Henly bought it in 1815. They sold the business to the Hudson's Bay Company in 1873. (Its initials HBC, locals contended, stood for Here Before Christ.) On Grenfell's first visit to the village in 1893, he found a few small houses and the Hudson's Bay Company station, a legacy of sorts from the settlement's founder.

Cartwright died in Nottinghamshire in 1819. His niece, Frances, put up a graceful white marble marker in the Labrador village's cemetery in memory of him and his brother, John. It reads: "In zealously protecting and befriending [they] paved the way of the introduction of Christianity to the natives of these benighted regions."

Cartwright harbor is a snug U lying on its side, its mouth facing westward to a magnificent view of Earl Island across Favorite Tickle with the Mealy Mountains looming behind the island. Most of the hamlet is spread along the north shore with the Grenfell mission opposite, a half-mile south. Hogarth Forsyth regretted the separation which required a boat ride for Cartwrighters to reach the hospital. It also effectively segregated us WOPs from most of the villagers for most of the summer.

We finally got to see the village on a short visit. It consisted mostly of compact, weathered clapboard bungalows, churches, the Hudson's Bay store, a small fish processing plant and a Royal Canadian Mounted Police office. Henry Gordon, who traveled the coast from Cartwright from 1915 to 1925, said living conditions in the village were "far superior to any of those" elsewhere in his parish district. This was due, he thought, to many of the local people being descendants of carpenters, coopers, tinsmiths and other craftsmen brought out by the early trading companies. They passed on their skills as well as customs and "pictures, rocking chairs and crockery, all reminiscent of some old English country cottage."

The mission buildings, utilitarian in design, neat and well maintained, were of white frame with dark green trim to make them more visible in blinding snowstorms. Straight up the hill from the dock was the Maclay Hospital. Off to the right was the school dormitory, the size and shape of a small barn. Between the hospital and the dorm was the Lockwood School, with four classrooms and a second-floor assembly room. On the slope toward the dock, along a gravel roadway, were a handicraft shop where products of the cottage industry were sold, a maintenance building and houses for the doctor and his wife, nurses and other staff.

We arrived at the harbor in early afternoon. George Swift was taken by boat to the mission wharf and thence to the hospital. We followed in the second boat, unpacked in the dormitory's second-floor, barracks-like bunk room and met teenage Jane and Iris (pronounced oiris), friendly girls given to gales of giggling, who would cook and wash clothes for us.

The next morning Charlie Bird, the mission's maintenance chief, who was to be our boss, came around and introduced himself. He was a short, stocky, middle-aged man whose eyes and complexion suggested a trace of Inuit ancestry. His habitual garb was a dark suit, white shirt, necktie and cap. Gordon described him as "a man of real vision as regards the future of Labrador [sharing] my own great hope for some improved system of education." Bird and Harry King did not hit it off. "He bullied the natives," King said years later. "He had patronage to dispense. His trouble was in dealing with college men." Ruprecht and I had no problems with him.

It was with Charlie that we began navigating our way in Labradorese, a variation of eighteenth century West-of-England dialects, much more pronounced in 1941 than now. "Oy" and "eye" sounds were reversed; "hide the toy" would come out "hoid t' ty." "Tide is out" was heard as "toid is oot." "Put the end in" became "Put un aind een." Outlanders "come from away." Occasionally was "scatter-time." As with Samuel Johnson, "sir" was interjected in conversation with a man. Women were often addressed as "m'dear."

Our first job, drably domestic, lasted only a couple of days: stacking cans of food in the dormitory's pantry. After that we got down to our first real work, building a road from the rear of the dorm sixty yards back to a shed. Work did not begin, however, until after a spirited argument between Harry

King and Charlie Bird about the roadway's route. Charlie, of course, prevailed. The plan was to dig out a level roadbed, then fill it with ballast and gravel. Labrador's flinty gneiss did not yield gently to our picks and shovels, but we completed the project in a couple of weeks.

Then came the summer's main task: laying in the 200 cords of wood fuel required by the hospital, school and dormitory for the long, cold winter. The routine began with a trip in an open boat manned by Harvey Bird, Charlie's son, or Mickey Bird, his nephew, to the head of Sandwich Bay. There we would find a jumble of black-spruce logs ten to twelve feet long that had been cut during the winter and spring. We would pitch them onto the boat for the 15-mile trip back to the dock where we would unload the logs on the wharf, then reload them onto the black Model-A Ford pickup, the same one the pipeline diggers had used in 1931.

The truck, which some believe was a gift of Henry Ford, a friend of Grenfell's, was then the only motor vehicle in all of Labrador, an expanse the size of Italy. With the truck we would haul the wood up the hill where we would lean the logs in three upright stacks. By the summer's end each stack, like a huge brown corn shock, was about thirty feet across. When we weren't stacking logs, we were cutting them by handsaw into fireplace lengths and piling them up in the dormitory's woodshed. In our last week or so of the firewood detail we were joined by William Max Asher, an easygoing, crew-cut medical student from Los Angeles. He had been busy most of the summer with medical duties on the *Maraval*, which had dropped him off at Cartwright to catch the *Kyle* to St. John's with us.

The work was simple, repetitious and physical but agreeable. By nightfall we were aware of well-used muscles. We were bothered by black flies and mosquitoes, but not to the point of the pipeline crew's distraction deep in the windless woods. What we did helped a good cause and robbed no Cartwrighters of work; every available hand was off fishing or berry picking. I had no sense of performing "missionary work," however. For me, the summer was simply an adventure.

Our meals were simple but hearty: oatmeal and bread for breakfast, plus a shot of lemon juice to ward off scurvy; a Sandwich Bay sandwich for lunch, and for dinner potato and turnip stews fortified with fish or rabbit, washed down by the ubiquitous Labrador tea, traditionally served "hot as hell, black as sin and sweet as love." King, bored by an overdose of Philadelphia talk between Ruprecht and me, took to reading *Anna Karenina* at the dinner table and finished it by the summer's end. It was chilly enough many evenings to light a fire in the dorm's cavernous stone fireplace.

George Swift's life, meanwhile, hung by a thread for a couple of weeks in the hospital. The chance for an appendectomy was long past; peritonitis had taken over. Dr. Forsyth inserted a tube in his abdomen to drain off poison, but it took no fewer than eight small operations to keep the drain functioning. He dosed his patient with sulfanilamide, fed him through a tube in an ankle vein and administered morphine when the pain became unbearable. "It was a blessing. Then I could get some sleep," Swift recalled long afterward. "My neighbor in the ward was a guy whose arm had been ripped up in a shotgun accident. He was in agony but he kept quiet. I wasn't very brave about pain. The care was superb. The nurses were great, very loving."

In a July 30, 1941, letter to Katie Spalding, the doctor wrote, "One of our WOPs arrived with a perforated appendix, and we had a terrific time pulling him through... I was going up to St. Anthony for Sir Wilf's funeral, but got stuck with the sick WOP, unfortunately."

When Swift finally was taken off intravenous feeding, he remembered Hazel Compton, the hospital's "big, fat, red-faced, jolly [full-time] nurse," bringing him hot cocoa after each of the eight drainage operations. "I'd be half out of it with ether, but I sure appreciated it." As his recovery gained momentum, he was graduated to soup and custards. We visited him from time to time as he improved, but spared him further readings from *Wuthering Heights*.

When we asked the doctor how his patient was doing, his standard answer, in clipped British, was, "Oh, not so dusty." For a while, we read him as the quintessential stiff-upper-lip Englishman, straight out of Central Casting. As the summer ran on, other facets of the Forsyth persona came to light. He was an admirer of Whitman's *Leaves of Grass*, a fan of the English composer Frederick Delius, records of whose music he played on his wind-up Victrola, and the leader of Sunday worship services. His calf-sized black Newfoundland dog, Royal, was the pet of the whole mission.

In later years, George Swift came to understand fully what a blessing the care of Forsyth, the nurses and the hospital had been for him. In the doctor's words, "There is not a town in the country of more than 250 people, but I venture to say that [we have] a 'modern' medical service." Maclay Hospital, he added, "is simply but completely equipped"—mobile x-ray unit with all accessories, "though many of these, from the table down, are homemade." The operating room's centerpiece was a pedestal operating table, "but the rest of its equipment is effective but inexpensive kitchen furniture... Dressing sterilization is done in a canning retort over a powerful petrol stove..."

One still, gray afternoon our routines were jolted by the arrival of an olive drab U.S. Navy PBY Catalina flying boat which floated down to a landing on the harbor, graceful as a swan, homely as a pelican, with a roar that brought people out of houses. Plane arrivals were then roughly as frequent as lunar eclipses. An anchor was dropped and the PBY's five occupants piled into a rubber dinghy and rowed over to our dock. First up the ladder was their leader, Army Air Corps Captain Elliott Roosevelt, the President's amiable, 30-year-old, 225-pound second son. He and his crew were to use Cartwright as a base from which to scout the area for the site of a touch-down airfield for planes being flown from the United States to England.

Roosevelt and his men—two Air Corps pilots, a navigator and a Navy officer from Boston who had worked with the Grenfell mission in the area—were lodged in the dorm with us. We ate together around a Ping-Pong table in the big first-floor dining room, bringing us a double bonus: a share of the juicy steaks they had brought with them, and Roosevelt's equally juicy conversation. We heard, for example, of a visit he and his wife, actress Faye Emerson, had made to the San Simeon castle of publisher William Randolph Hearst; of swimming in an indoor pool lined, he said, with lapis lazuli (actually, blue Venetian-glass tiles); of suppers in the baronial dining room, hung with flags and lit by four-foot silver candlesticks. Hearst's mistress, the movie star Marion Davies, had persuaded the butler to fill her water glass with straight gin, our visitor said, thus surreptitiously eluding Hearst's ban on her drinking. Exotic chat for us young provincials.

He and his team flew out of Cartwright every morning for several days, then got fogged in for a couple more before leaving. The site they chose became, in a relatively short time, Goose Bay airfield. Hundreds of England-bound planes stopped there during the war, and the field remains Labrador's central air terminal. Forty years later, in a phone conversation from his home in Bellevue, Washington, Roosevelt talked about his assignment and its several goals.

"We were looking for solid ground in an uninhabited area," he said. "And we needed a lot of land," because of the heavy weight of the planes and the long runways they required. "We spent two days, after borrowing some boats, to get to an area we had reconnoitered by air. We beat our way through tundra to get to a high plateau. We had to find out how much level land there was, and when we got there it looked good. Then we took some more pictures by air. On the last day the Canadians came in. They were miffed that we had beaten them to choosing the site."

The location he had picked was on a twelve-square-mile plateau, some of which was known locally as Uncle Bob's Berry Patch, since Robert Michelin collected redberries there. The plateau, of sand 700 feet deep left by the last ice age, had no barriers to flight in any direction. The United States and Canada built the airfield, leaving enough acreage for Uncle Bob to continue harvesting berries. It was used even by fighter planes headed for Europe. Pilots flew a rough great-circle route from Goose Bay to Greenland's east coast to Iceland to England, Roosevelt said.

Fifty years later, in 1991, I flew up to Goose Bay after a visit to Cartwright. The town, then numbering 7,500 people, was energetically celebrating its fiftieth anniversary. A beach festival, air show and canoe regatta were scheduled for "Fifty Years on the Goose." Ironically, in none of newspapers or handouts that I saw was there any mention of Elliott Roosevelt's coming upon Uncle Bob's berry patch in the summer of 1941 which had led to Goose Bay's founding. Maybe I had missed it in earlier issues. Then again, maybe Goose Bayers were not anxious to recognize an American hand in their corporate origin. It made me feel that I had witnessed history from behind the door.

Roosevelt's team also had been told to locate a German radio station in eastern Greenland which was giving vital weather information to U-boats. "We found it, flew over it and gave its exact location," he said. "The British later captured and destroyed it." Finally, he and his crew went on to Baffin Island and Elesmere Island in the far north to select locations for three weather stations to give the British advance information on weather systems moving toward them. "We located the proper areas with good potential for air and water weather stations," he said.

Roosevelt—he was a twice-wounded major general by the end of the war—was stationed at the time at Gander field in

Newfoundland, assigned to an air reconnaissance squadron. With his Labrador mission completed, he got orders to pick up an "important person" flying into Gander. This turned out to be Lord Beaverbrook, Churchill's supply minister. He was headed to the August 14 meeting of his boss and President Roosevelt, aboard the U.S. cruiser *Augusta* and the British battleship *Prince of Wales*, off Argentia in Newfoundland's Placentia Bay. It was the first international conference an American president had ever held at sea. The President leaned on Elliott's arm as he met with the Prime Minister at what became known as the Atlantic Charter conference where the alliance's global aims were set.

Cartwright's other notable visitor that summer was George Swift's mother, Mrs. Cornelia Wagstaff. Forsyth had cabled Grenfell headquarters to send word to her that George was "gravely ill." The intended implication was that she should be prepared for his death. She left immediately and came up as we had, but with a hair-raising passage through the Strait of Belle Isle. It occurred at night in fog, and this time the *Kyle* encountered two convoys headed in opposite directions, again with lights blacked out because of the U-boat danger. The captain ordered everyone on deck in life jackets. She could make out the inky outlines of freighters churning by in the murk like charging black bulls. Twice the *Kyle*'s engines had to be violently reversed to avoid a collision. She reached Cartwright safely, however, a couple of weeks after our arrival.

No doctor could have prescribed better convalescence therapy than Cornelia Scranton Wagstaff. Perennially buoyant, a joke seemed always ready to explode behind her brown eyes. Buck-toothed, rosy-cheeked and pencil-thin, aged 45 when we met her, she dressed most of the time in jodhpurs, a tweed riding jacket and brown felt hat, trappings of a fox hunting life on Long Island. She was a first cousin of William Scranton, later governor of Pennsylvania and a Republican presidential aspirant. In addition to her bonhomie, she brought with her cans of fruit juice and tomato juice for George and some books: Joseph Lincoln's Cape Cod stories and Kipling's *Captains Courageous*. "It was a great comfort having her there," Swift recalled.

Our contacts with her included evening "mug-ups" of tea at the hospital with her and the nurses and occasional poker games. These were usually joined by Dr. Crenshaw who clearly had learned the game around some testing tables in South Carolina. His demeanor was unchanged regardless of the cards he held: breezily confident. Thus, he would give us tyros not the slightest clue that behind his sure-thing bets lay a jack-high hand. The stakes were small but he cleaned up. On the way back to the dorm after such evenings, if it was clear, we would watch, mesmerized, the ghostly wave of aurora borealis, fingers of gauzy white and green light reaching across the star-crusted sky.

One mission staff person who did not join in our recreations was Mrs. Kate M. Keddie. She held the imposing title of production director of the Industrial Department at Cartwright. That meant that she got materials around to householders in the area and then collected and sent on to stores the garments, carvings, mats and such that they made. Short, stocky and taciturn, with a broad, smiling face, Kitty Keddie had come out of The Pas, a northern Manitoba village. She is described by one Grenfell biographer as "an old sweetheart" of the doctor's.

Mrs. Keddie, then in her mid-40s, padded around the mission in sneakers, from her small shop/supply room to her bungalow, which had been set on logs and rolled by the tractor from back in the woods to the mission's main street. Technically, she was our other boss, along with Charlie Bird, but we heard little from her. Nor did we gauge the pioneering heart beneath the placid exterior. This was no little old lady in sneakers. Here is a Keddie letter to Grenfell, dated January 5, 1935:

"I have been away all week on a trip around the bay. Visited every house. We the first team to get into Dove Brook, ice very poor; our dogs got into the water and we were lucky not to go in too. Soon after reaching Dove Brook, storm broke in a perfect fury, piling up snow in huge mountains of drift.

"House I was staying at was completely blocked, had to be shoveled out. Stormbound for three days, then went on to White Bear River, Eagle River, Separation Point, Paradise Arm, Longstretch, Muddy Brook, then home. I was able to give out a lot of industrial work. I am leaving for another trip in about ten days, visiting Sandy Hills and that part."

"I had been worried for several days after my return from Porcupine Bay," she added, "as some families down there are absolutely destitute. It is appalling to see a family of five children get up in the morning and there is no breakfast to give them and no prospect for dinner, yet that is how I found one family and others like it."

Our summer's off-hours apex was a fishing trip on a brilliant late summer Sunday to the Eagle River at the head of the bay, very much like the Pumphrey crew's with Grenfell. The expedition included Crenshaw, Mrs. Wagstaff, Miss MacDonald, the assistant nurse, and us WOPs, except for Swift. Having been equipped with rods, reels and the rest, we were taken up-bay in the mission's open boat by Harvey Bird. There we were joined by a guide who steered us down a dirt road to a boiling rapids near a pool named for George Cartwright. Sea trout were running and we caught a few, some a foot and a half long and game fighters. One, hooked above the rapids, took me stumbling through brush and rocks down past the rapids before being landed in a calmer stretch below.

That section of the Eagle River, it turned out, was (and remains) famous fishing water. William O. Brown, a long-time guide on the river, years later accompanied Prince Philip there once, and American Air Force General Curtis "Ironpants" LeMay frequently. The biggest fish Brown ever saw caught in the river was a 32-pound salmon landed by George Williams, of the Williams shaving cream family. Williams had a cabin near the rapids and came up summers on his schooner. Today more than a dozen fishing camps for affluent sportsmen are strung along the river.

Another excursion was less fulfilling. One Sunday, Ruprecht and I, perhaps inspired by Grenfell's polar-bear plunges, decided to try a swim. We borrowed a boat, rowed out into the harbor, stripped to trunks and dove in. The dive and the scramble out of the breath-stopping water and back into the boat were all a single move. George Cartwright to the contrary, we did not feel "as if we had shot within the tropics."

We had not come to Labrador for cultural enrichment but found some anyway—in listening to the Delius records at the Forsyths' on our few visits there, and in another surprising discovery. In a corner of the dorm's dining room was a standing windup vic of curving architecture, a gift no doubt of some mission beneficiary. Behind its cabinet doors was a small collection of Victor Red Seal records, including one of the only opera aria I had ever heard at that point, a lilting duet by Enrico Caruso and Ernestine Schumann-Heink of "Ai Nostri Monti" (Home to Our Mountains) from Verdi's *Il Trovatore*. This in Cartwright, Labrador. We gave the Red Seals a workout.

The relative harmony among us working WOPs was seriously disrupted only once during the summer. Harry King's dark hair was beginning to thin on top, and at age twenty this disturbed him. Someone told him that the fish plant across the harbor, in producing cod liver oil, created a byproduct that could grow hair on a doorknob. It was an opportunity that Moose could not resist. He got hold of a jar of this foul elixir, smeared it on his scalp, donning a stocking cap before retiring. Even with the windows wide open, the place stank like the hold of a Gloucester smack. We stood the stench for a night before delivering an ultimatum: the fish goo went or he did. Reluctant and protesting, he gave in. The experiment's intriguing coda was that his thatch, forty years later, may not have sprouted like spring grass but it didn't seem to have lost a hair since Labrador.

Of the general instructions the Association gave its volunteers, the most emphatic dealt with alcohol. Noting that "Dr. Grenfell was largely instrumental in bringing Prohibition to Newfoundland," the directions added: "It is essential that no one attached in any way to the Grenfell Mission shall drink alcoholic liquors of any kind while on the way to or from his or her post, as well as while on the Coast. The fact that a worker has signed an application form is considered a pledge that this regulation will be upheld." The night before departure on the *Kyle*, George Swift and his mother were invited to the Forsyths' for dinner. The doctor offered Mrs. Wagstaff a cocktail, and her 17-year-old son asked if he could have one, too. Regulations or not, their host poured his patient a whiskey. "You've been through hell," he said. "You were fine." Swift downed it appreciatively.

In an account of her trip in the mission's journal, *Among the Deep Sea Fishers*, Mrs. Wagstaff wrote of their departure: "As we turned out of the bight [on the *Kyle*], I stood by the rail with a lump in my throat and watched Cartwright slowly disappearing. I realized that if it had not been George's good fortune to have the efficient surgeon and splendid nurses of the Grenfell hospital at Cartwright looking after him day and night for weeks, I might have been taking that trip back to the States alone."

The trip down was simpler and quicker than the one north. No ice fields, no train rides. At St. John's we transferred onto a larger ship, the *Fort Townsend*, which took us in comfort direct to New York. Samuel Wagstaff, George's stepfather, met the ship at the dock. As we waited to debark, he shouted up to his wife, "The price of whiskey has gone up."

We were back in what some might call the real world.

7 From Pueblo to Park Avenue

A favorite Grenfell story about volunteers had as its heroine "Nurse Jardine"—Marjory Jardine, of Toronto, a nurse at Massachusetts General Hospital in Boston. She served unpaid at St. Anthony in 1918-19.

The story, which illustrates the extremes of service volunteers sometimes performed, is more accurately told by Jardine herself (later Mrs. Harvey Armstrong) in a May 1919 letter home:

Dr. Charles Curtis, medical director at the station, had gone to Conche on the "French Shore" 65 miles south, on a case and found so much influenza that he wired for a nurse to come down and help out. The first part of Jardine's adventure was the three-day trip to Conche, a bit more involved than your basic house call.

She and the mission's driver, Alec Simms, start out with a dog team "with our eyes well goggled for snow blindness." After traveling all day, they reach Island Rock Cove and are taken in by hospitable people in a log cabin. "I slept in a little room just off the kitchen," she wrote, "and was awakened early by the cackling hens and crowing roosters who slept in the kitchen..." At Island Rock Cove she meets Curtis coming north by boat and she exchanges the komatik for his boat and its crew of five men. By motor and sail they head for the Fishot Islands "but were cut off by the ice and had to make a quick landing for our lives from the pans of ice" on a rocky cape called Maiden's Harbor.

They don't know where they are but start walking inland "through brooks, ponds and rivers and forests" with snow and rain falling. They finally reach another log house and again are taken in by a hospitable family. She and her overweight hostess share a small bed. Up at 5 a.m., they start early and reach Conche after changing dog teams three times.

There she finds six "very sick" people including Peter, "my star patient." "Easter Monday morning," she wrote, "a hurry call came for me and I dashed up to the house where the accident happened. Found a man [Peter] unconscious from loss of blood, having a severe traumatic wound in the abdomen, the large intestine hanging out, from a sealing knife..." As she arrives at his home, Father Thibault, the Roman Catholic parish priest, is administering last rites "as the man was almost gone, while I cut off his clothes." Down with influenza and delirious with a high fever, he had wandered at night to the hayloft of his barn and ripped himself up.

Having nothing sterile at hand, she uses a hot salt solution and boiled table napkins for first aid while some of the men put up a bed. "I put some hypos into him in double quick time but truly never expected to get him into bed alive," she wrote. Finding internal bleeding and hemorrhaging, "the only thing to do was operate."

She desperately wires Dr. Curtis for instructions but couldn't get a reply fast enough so, with the family's consent, she decides to go ahead with the operation. Again Fr. Thibault gives last rites. "Fortunately, I had a few clamps, scissors and cat gut to sew with. By this time Peter was becoming conscious and very restless, so that I had to give him ether..." The priest takes over anesthesia while she scrubs up. "I put back the intestines," she continued, "tied off the arteries, put a rubber drain in and packed the abdomen with a cheesecloth sugar bag and sutured up, only having to get unsterile once to give a hypo, as he stopped breathing altogether and was pulseless. Here I almost died, too."

"Complications" follow, probably infection, because of the dirty sealing knife and the hayloft where the injury happened. "But he lives!" she wrote triumphantly. "Dr. Grenfell is sure he will have a crop of hay around the wound." Then comes the journey to St. Anthony to continue the patient's recovery in the hospital.

They rig up a tent and stoves on a motor boat for Peter and another stretcher patient. All goes well until they run into an ice jam at Goose Cove, seven miles from St. Anthony, and have to switch to dog teams. Snow is patchy and "the dogs had a hard pull, and the patients [too]. I tried to steady the komatik over some of the rocks... The trip did not do Peter any good as he was pretty weak and the bumps extremely hard. However, under the hospital roof he has picked up a good deal. We are great friends..." By the end of the summer he is back in his boat fishing.

> "When I had finished recounting this story [at Massachusetts General]," Grenfell wrote, "half the nurses in the hospital wanted to go to Labrador on the next boat."

WOPs were jacks of many trades. Lone young women taught small roomfuls of kids their ABCs and how to brush their teeth. As many as a score of college men would be enlisted for big construction projects in a time and place where human labor was the common denominator. Other WOPs did stevedore work, shoveling coal and hoisting cargo on ships. The job that occupied many of the land-based crews, as it had us in Cartwright, was bringing in tons of firewood against the oncoming chill of the Labrador winter.

Sometimes they did work that would be unthinkable today for the medically untrained. Bevan Pumphrey tells of a short stop at the mission's station at Twillingate, Newfoundland, on the way up to Cartwright in 1931. The surgeon there jumped to the assumption that the young English WOP was a medical student. "They had a surgeon's coat round me, a white skull cap on my head and a mask over my mouth before I could adequately protest," he wrote later. With probable exaggeration, he added: "Within a matter of minutes I was assisting at what proved to be the first of twenty-seven major operations in three days... I was once even given the responsibility of acting as anesthetist [during an appendectomy]. The surgeons worked on this patient (a woman) for nearly an hour and half, during which time I regulated the flow of ether according to the pulse as felt by my little finger on the temporal artery, the rate being called out at minute intervals... One felt thankful that she knew so little."

The building of a new 70-bed hospital at St. Anthony in the mid-1920s involved major volunteer effort. WOPs cleared the site, dug and built the foundations and, with professional supervision and local workers, erected the steel and concrete walls. An American volunteer architect, William A. Delano, had designed the buildings. Thirty years later, in the construction of a new hospital at North West River, volunteers shoveled hundreds of tons of concrete makings into and out of barges and hauled lumber and other supplies to the site. A travail only slightly less epic than the pipeline dig at Cartwright was construction of a reservoir with a half-mile ditch to bring piped water to the hospital at St. Anthony.

In 1929 at Cartwright, a gang of ten WOPs helped clear and level the site for the station's buildings. "Supervisor of outdoor workers" there that summer was Hanson W. Baldwin, a graduate of the Naval Academy five years earlier, who had served three years in the Navy. After his Labrador summer he joined *The New York Times* staff and later became one of its premier war correspondents, winning a Pulitzer Prize in 1943 for a series of articles on the conflict in the South Pacific. He served as the *Times*'s military news editor until retirement in 1968.

Another account of volunteer enterprise that appealed to Grenfell involved the hard-nosed skipper of a merchant vessel delivering 400 tons of coal to St. Anthony. The cargo had to be unloaded in three days, he told the mission. After that, a heavy daily demurrage charge would be levied. A sweating gang of back-weary WOPs wielded shovels more than twelve hours a day to move the coal from hold to dock by the end of the third day.

"Roads, water supplies, wharves, land clearing, buildings," the doctor said in a 1934 London broadcast, "besides medical, surgical, child welfare, industrial, social, agricultural—indeed the greater part of our work would never have been possible except for these volunteers."

The sentiment was echoed half a century later by Dr. W. Anthony Paddon, medical officer at North West River for thirty-one years. "Through all my years at North West River," he wrote, "the work of the Grenfell mission would simply have been impossible without the efforts of the volunteers."

The term WOP, according to the latest and best of Grenfell's biographers, Ronald G. Rompkey, originated in a conversation between the missionary and "a spoiled young man who felt superior to the work [and] deemed it fit only for 'wops,' as the Italian laborers in the United States were known. Grenfell replied that in Labrador everybody was a wop and did his or her share of useful labor. Henceforth, all volunteers were known by the term, even though Grenfell later tried to suggest that it was an acronym for 'without pay.'" The acronym explanation was the one we were given.

The Venerable Robert A. Bryan, an Episcopal priest who ran the mission's volunteer program in the latter half of the 1960s, purged the moniker, and substituted the cumbersome but more apt "Grenfell summer volunteer." "I was appalled that even in the mid-60s we had that name," said Bryan. "It's an ethnic slur. Some of the Boston Brahmins got upset with me for changing it. I said, no way I can recruit on campuses and use the word WOP."

W. B. Wakefield may have been the first Grenfell volunteer, but Clark Munden, a deckhand on the *Strathcona* in the summer of 1903, was the first to make it into the mission's records. He was followed in 1905 by a couple of surgeons from Boston hospitals. By 1938, two years before he died, Grenfell put the volunteer total at 2,000. Dr. Gordon Thomas, IGA executive director during most of the 1960s and '70s, estimated the number of volunteers from 1940 to 1976, when the movement was ended, at about 1,500.

The sum of the two estimates, 3,500, almost exactly corresponds to the number I dredged up in a survey of the IGA index card file at St. Anthony. The file shows about 2,800 WOPs, of whom 89 percent came from the United States, and 700 volunteer medical students, nurses, doctors and dentists.

Mission records began clearly differentiating staff from volunteers only in 1929. The decade of the 1930s was a big volunteer era for the IGA despite the worldwide depression. Mission annals for the decade show a total of 697 of the uncompensated, of whom 609, or 87 percent, were Americans. Six percent were English or Scottish and 5 percent Canadian. Two-thirds of the Americans came from—in this order—Massachusetts, New York, Pennsylvania, New Jersey and Connecticut. The lion's share of the volunteer corps were WOPs—workers and teachers—564 out of the total 697 (81 percent).

Some came from tony addresses—the Chestnut Hills of Philadelphia and Massachusetts, Park Avenue and Newport. For a few women in the debutante set, WOP work was chic. "You'd read in the social columns [in New York] that so-and-so of the Junior League spent the summer at the Grenfell mission," recalled Eleanor Cushman Wescott, Sir Wilfred's secretary for eight years and IGA executive secretary for eighteen more. But other volunteers hailed from far less fashionable locales like Petoskey, Michigan; Dysart, Iowa; Pueblo, Colorado. Seven WOPs in that decade made it from Milwaukee, six from California. Still others traveled global distances to work on the Coast: from Tasmania below Australia; Auckland, New Zealand, and Alexandria, Egypt.

One devoted ophthalmologist, Dr. Joseph Andrews, came to St. Anthony from Santa Barbara by train and ship for eighteen straight years, beginning in 1909, to offer his services free.

Until 1928, the Grenfell Association identified WOPs by their college or school. Then, perhaps realizing that they might be embarrassing unaffiliated volunteers, they switched to listing only home addresses. Among the colleges, Yale, Harvard and Princeton—"the Big Three" in those days—were heavily represented. But WOPs came, too, from more modest campuses like Trinity in Hartford and Swarthmore in Pennsylvania, from Philadelphia's Pierce Business College and Lake Erie College in Painesville, Ohio.

Money sometimes followed volunteer work. By 1923, thirteen medical students of Columbia's College of Physicians and Surgeons had worked summers on Spotted Island off the Labrador coast. They had also erected a ward building and a combination school, church and recreation center and had given a launch to take the med students on professional visits to other islands. Yale students, or more likely their families, donated a 44-foot ketch to the North West River station. The vessel became Dr. Harry Paddon's first medical boat. They also raised enough money to build a school at the station. Occasionally, Grenfell observed, male WOPs serving on mission ships "have taken back some of their shipmates to the United States for a year's education."

A few volunteers even found true love on the coast. Lisa Simonds, a 20-year-old Smith senior from Greenwich, Connecticut, was helping in the Grenfell hospital at North West River in 1950 when she met her future husband. Edwin Maynard, 24, from Brooklyn, a medical student at the College of Physicians and Surgeons, walked into the hospital carrying a raincoat she had left at Goose Bay airport, and that lit the fire. He spent the summer on the *Maraval* pulling teeth, delivering babies and anesthetizing surgery patients. He went on to become an internist at Massachusetts General Hospital. The couple settled down in Chestnut Hill near Boston to rear their four children.

Early on, the founder himself selected the WOPs. "It will be a great pleasure to me to have Nelson and Laurance on the boat," Grenfell told John D. Rockefeller Jr., their father, in a hand-written letter of May 14, 1929. The previous December, he had written him, "I hope you will tell the boys that we expect them to work just as well as if they were paid crew." It was a rare WOP family that received the chief's personal attention, of course, and the reason for that particular exception may be guessed. Some years later the International Grenfell Association was pleased to report that John's wife had contributed a "large sum." Hefty enough, in fact, that the mere interest from it contributed substantially toward purchase of a 145-foot ship.

Pumphrey tells of his own interview by Grenfell in 1930 in the doctor's study at Magdalen College, Oxford.

"You belong to the Quakers? Splendid," the missionary began. "Have you done anything you shouldn't lately?"

"I was in serious trouble earlier in the term," replied the youth, then a sixth-former in school at Reading, "for flying over the school and persuading the pilot to do aerobatics directly over the buildings."

"That is excellent," came the response. "I will recommend our Selection Committee to accept you for the coming year." The selection committee, before whom Pumphrey duly appeared, consisted of one person: Grenfell.

But having the all-embracing doctor—often an easy target for a hard-luck story—choose volunteer workers had its hazards. Occasionally, the father of a son abusing alcohol or drugs would ask Grenfell to take the youth as a WOP to straighten him out. Almost without exception, the doctor assented.

Eleanor Wescott said a western Massachusetts psychiatric hospital "used to advise its [patients] to go up to the Coast. These people were not out of control but they needed help. We would offer them jobs." Grenfell viewed their inclusion as part of his healing ministry. "Nervous breakdown patients..." he wrote, "responded... to the 'Labrador treatment.'" They were a tiny fraction of the whole, he said. He also claimed apocryphally that, for everyone accepted in the WOP program, two were rejected.

Some of the mission's doctors, including Curtis, who were on the receiving end of problem WOPs, finally put a foot down. The number of volunteers was cut and the screening process passed to a real selection committee. Applicants had to produce two references and a doctor's certificate of their fitness ("none but those capable of steady, arduous work should apply"), and come to New York or Boston, if possible, for an interview. Even then, "we didn't turn down too many," Mrs. Wescott said. Those who were accepted signed a contract.

The volunteers received a sheet of information and instructions, which included the ban on alcohol in transit or on the coast. Women were asked not to smoke in public. Vassar women were barred from mission work for a time. The captain of the ship bringing them north complained that they had smoked and behaved in an "objectionable way."

Since people on the coast generally were religious and God-fearing, volunteers were urged to observe the Sabbath. "The Mission does not ask anyone to go to church against his will, but it does suggest that in this, as in other ways of keeping Sunday, a friendly relation can be cultivated." Far from urging WOPs not to leave home without traveler's checks, the mission declared that on the Coast they "have no value... It must be cash." Men were told to bring a dark suit and light shirts for Sunday use, "working gloves, plenty of socks and hip-length rubber boots." The boots mandate was ignored by many, including us at Cartwright. The first boat north left St. John's in early June, the sheet noted, and the summer's last boat south docked at the capital in the last week of October.

Grenfell rejoiced in the idea of voluntarism as a demonstration of sacrificial self-giving. Usually, he liked WOPs and enjoyed their company. But at times, especially in his later years, they got under his skin. "I do my best to keep young," he wrote his wife plaintively from shipboard in 1927, "but the crew gets on my nerves. One is *never* alone, and the boys... are so much at home that they use everything you have and sit in your seat and have dirty clothes anywhere & even now have natives in my cabin to show them movie pictures 'downstairs.' You see you *must* keep them satisfied or it would be worse." Nor was he enchanted with their culinary skills. "I don't really take chances on my boat," he wrote on another occasion, "except that I do carry a volunteer cook from Harvard or Yale or some other college. Maybe that's one of the greatest risks I ever took on the sea."

Two of the Cartwright pipeline trench diggers hard at daunting work.

The 1931 crew pouring concrete for the Burdett's Brook dam.

Raymond Humphrey in 1920, sitting on the dam-he and colleagues helped build.

Sir Wilfred Grenfell and a young patient on his hospital ship.

Volunteer nurse Marjory Jardine off on a medical trip via dog team, circa 1918.

Courtesy of the Grenfell Historical Society

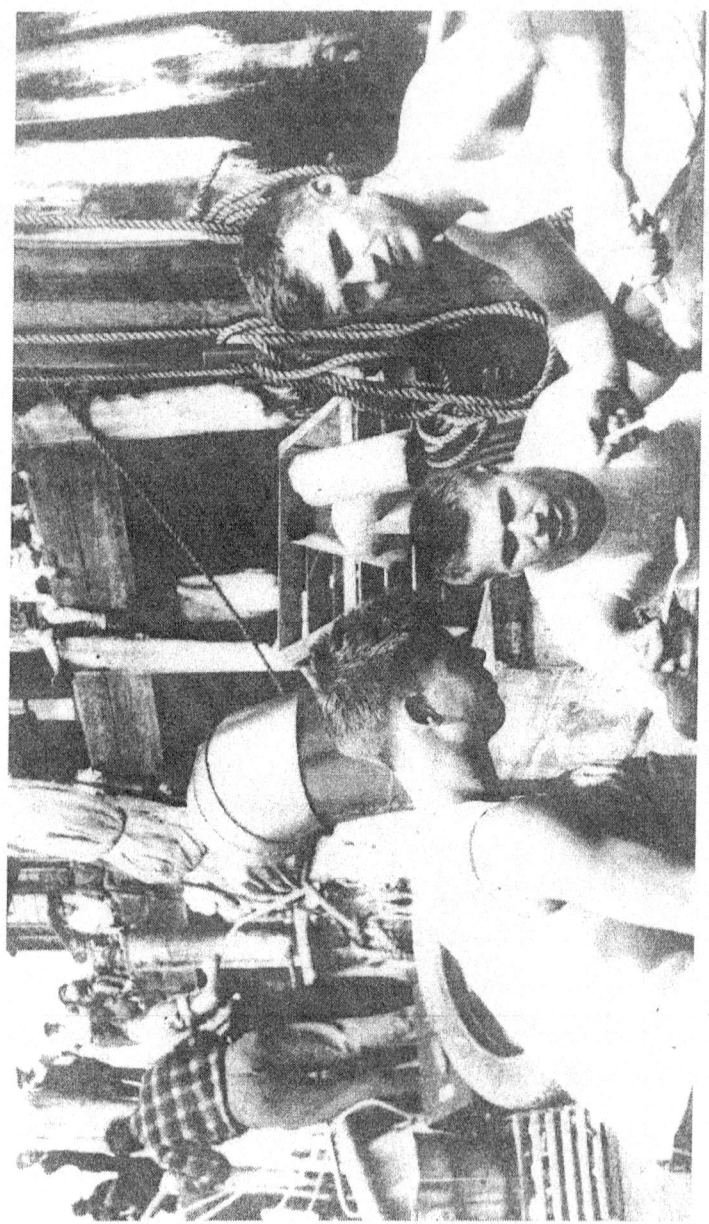

A crew-cut Nelson Rockefeller, center, eating lunch aboard the Grenfell hospital ship *Maraval* with two unidentified volunteers.

Courtesy of the Rockefeller Archive Center

Lockwood School and its dormitory with massive firewood stacks ready for winter in 1941.

Bill Asher stacking firewood logs in 1941 in Cartwright.

Dr. Hogarth Forsyth on board the *S. S. Kyle* in Cartwright harbor.

Dr. John Crenshaw, Forsyth's assistant.

Seated on the Model A pickup, 1941 Cartwright WOPs, from left, Harry Toland, Arch Ruprecht, Harry King.

Cartwright field day 1936: girls' 100-yard dash started by a Mountie's pistol shot.

Wilfred T. Grenfell Papers, Manuscripts & Archives, Yale University Library

8 Sketches

Volunteer work may have plugged a manpower gap for the Grenfell Mission, but for the volunteers what was it? An interesting summer adventure that gave them something to talk about back home? A toilful but mind-opening experience that in some way changed lives? A chance to serve people who needed a hand? A window onto how the world's other half—other 90 percent, rather—lived? Or perhaps an amalgam of the above along with a mysterious ingredient that has been called "the Grenfell." It depended on the individual, of course, and what happened to him or her on the coast and afterward. Here is a sampler.

FRANCIS B. SAYRE, who became the United States' last High Commissioner of the Philippines, was the WOP closest to Wilfred Grenfell. "One of my best friends," the missionary called him.

As a junior at Williams College, Sayre had read about the doctor, and invited him to address the student body. The day he visited the campus, he and the young undergraduate took an all-afternoon hike in the woods. "No one I had ever met impressed me so deeply," Sayre wrote later. He promised Grenfell he would work on the coast, and set about raising money for his mission.

That summer—1908—he and a Williams classmate, Douglas Palmer, fulfilled the promise. By then, there were hospitals at St. Anthony, Newfoundland, and at Harrington, Battle Harbor and Indian Harbor on the Labrador coast and a nursing station at Forteau, Labrador. Sayre cruised on the *Strathcona* for a couple of days with Grenfell and then was deposited at St. Anthony where he unloaded ships, did construction work, cut kids' hair at the Grenfell orphanage and even assisted in a couple of operations in the hospital. At the end of the summer he and a fellow volunteer, Scoville Clark, set out on foot to cross Newfoundland's boggy, lake-strewn upper peninsula. They trudged up to Cape Norman at the peak of the finger's west coast, then down to Flower's Cove, a hike of about seventy miles. Their food ran perilously low, and the black flies made a meal of them. "Our faces streamed with blood," he wrote.

At his graduation the following June, Sayre persuaded Williams's trustees to confer an honorary degree on Grenfell. The doctor came down to receive it and listen to his young friend deliver the valedictory.

That summer and the next, lugging a primitive typewriter, the hawk-nosed, gimlet-eyed Sayre sailed up and down the Newfoundland and Labrador coasts with his mentor on the *Strathcona*. He was the doctor's personal secretary, typing letters and copying manuscripts, but also helping in the sick bay and dispensing used clothing. He gladly joined the missionary in his dawn dives into the icy sea. "To him, his work and his religion were one... joyful service of Jesus Christ."

Robert Peary, returning from his claimed discovery of the North Pole in 1909, visited with Grenfell at Battle Harbor on the Labrador coast. Sayre found him "tall, stalwart, large-featured, with blue eyes and heavy blond mustache, his face seamed and gaunt from the grueling trip over the ice to the top of the world." At the explorer's request, the volunteer joined him to help transcribe his notes and records. He was with Peary aboard the *Roosevelt*, festooned with musk ox heads drying in the rigging, when the ship steamed through New York's Upper Bay to a whistle-blasting welcome.

On three occasions Grenfell tried to persuade Sayre to join him full time on the coast and "share the direction of his work." "Dear old Frank... I would just give almost my right hand to have you say, 'I'll come,'" he wrote in 1911. But the young man, then in Harvard Law School, after much soul-searching "chose New York" instead. He wasn't a doctor, he reasoned, and if serving mankind was "the prime objective, was it fair to choose Labrador with its thousands rather than New York with its millions?"

Born in South Bethlehem, Pennsylvania, Sayre was the son of a vice president of Bethlehem Iron Co. (later Bethlehem Steel) and president of the Lehigh Valley Railroad. The young man was well connected; he landed his first job as deputy assistant district attorney of New York with the help of Theodore Roosevelt. He was also wealthy enough to make a contribution to the Grenfell mission that allowed for doubling the capacity of the St. Anthony orphanage to forty children.

In November 1909, the young volunteer was an usher at Grenfell's wedding. The doctor reciprocated as best man at his friend's 1913 marriage to the radiant Jessie Woodrow Wilson, the President's daughter, in the White House. Fifty Newfoundland-Labrador acquaintances of the groom, including mission staffers, were invited to the ceremony.

In a foretaste of paparazzi frenzy, a $1,000 reward had been offered to any reporter who tracked the newlyweds after the wedding. Grenfell, at 48 still the zestful gamesman, had "heaps of fun" helping the bride and groom elude the newshounds. He arranged for a convoy of decoy automobiles to arrive at the White House's front entrance while a lone car picked up the honeymoon-bound couple at the south basement door.

After teaching at Harvard Law School with Felix Frankfurter, Sayre served for seven years in the 1920s as adviser to the Siamese government, then became an assistant secretary of state. Franklin Roosevelt appointed him High Commissioner of the Philippines in 1939. When the Japanese invaded the islands he and his second wife, Elizabeth, (Jessie had died in 1933) and her stepson took refuge in the Malinta Tunnel on Corregidor Island on Christmas Eve, 1941. With them were General Douglas MacArthur and Philippines President Manuel Quezon and their families and staffs. There they waited out two months of bombings and shellings, as the general oversaw the defense of the Bataan peninsula. With MacArthur seeing them off, the Sayres were evacuated at night on the submarine *Swordfish* and taken to Australia. Two weeks later MacArthur and his family and staff left by PT boat, also for Australia.

Sayre became diplomatic adviser to the United Nations Relief and Rehabilitation Administration (UNRRA) in 1944. During three years of shuttling 98,000 miles around the world, he raised more than $97 million to help feed and supply people ravaged by World War II, almost $1,000 per mile. In the early 1950s he spent two years in Japan as the personal representative of the Presiding Bishop of the Episcopal Church in an often frustrating effort to bring Christianity to the country's "laboring population." He died in 1972 at age 86.

He was convinced, he wrote, that Grenfell's influence in the United States—raising consciousness about the needy and recruiting volunteers to help them—was as important as his work in the north.

ELLIOTT T. MERRICK was 24 and two years out of Yale when he spent the summer of 1929 as a WOP at the station at Indian Harbor, a treeless, windswept rock island whose most prominent skyline resembled the profile of an Indian. It was a centuries-old summer gathering place of fishing schooners and formerly of whalers. The ships' crews were the bulk of the hospital's patients.

In later years, Merrick authored seven books, three of them about Labrador. He described his most vivid experience that summer in *Among the Deep Sea Fishers*: placing a stretcher-bound patient from the cottage hospital aboard the *Kyle* at night during a cold, driving rainstorm.

The patient, a Captain Willett, suffering from painful rheumatism and a heart problem, was being sent home by Dr. Harry Paddon. Paddon alternated as medical officer between Indian Harbor in the summer and North West River the rest of the year. The *Kyle*, skippered then by an intrepid Captain Clark, usually showed up at Indian Harbor in the middle of the night, fair weather or foul. The job of Merrick, who came from Montclair, New Jersey, and his fellow WOP, William Wetherill, of Philadelphia, was to make sure that patients got aboard safely.

That night the ship arrived at about midnight with the storm at full force. The two WOPs rolled Willett onto a stretcher as gently as they could although he was hurting, covered him with a canvas tarp and carried him down to an open fishing boat rocking at the dock. They laid the stretcher athwart the gunnels. With Paddon, the two volunteers, a medical student and a boat handler aboard, they set out for the *Kyle*, rolling in the billows beyond the harbor.

"We rounded the stern," Merrick wrote, "and came up to the companion ladder on the port side. 'Shut 'er off,' Doctor called. We drifted in and our coiled painter sailed over the rail and hit the deck with a satisfying thwack. A sailor ran forward with it and brought us alongside the companionway, which was banging viciously.

"'Watch your feet,' the sailor shouted. The boat rose halfway up the wooden stairway, then sank six feet below the bottom step. Clark's huge head and shoulders loomed over the bridge wing above. 'Go for'r'd and we'll hoist your man with the tackle,' he yelled.

"The sailor on deck hauled us forward, passing our painter outside each stanchion as he went. When we were abreast of the hatch, the cargo boom swung over, the winch rattled and the hook descended, a chain barrel sling dangling from it.

"With four doubles of codline we lashed each corner of the stretcher to the barrel sling. The bo's'n stood above holding the winch cable out from the ship's side. 'Come up easy,' he sang, and Captain Willett was whisked to the deck as smooth as glass."

Merrick and Wetherill went aboard, carried the patient aft to the steerage cabin and warped him gingerly into a bunk.

"When it was over he sighed with relief. 'You're a pair o' manhandlers all right,' he grinned. 'You lay another finger on me and I'll pitch you overboard, the two of ye.' He had sand and no mistake."

At other times, Merrick and Wetherill hoisted freight from the *Strathcona's* hold, lowered it to a dory, rowed it ashore and carried it up the hill; whitewashed the hospital, patched the roof, split wood for the stoves that heated the two wards (with a dozen patients in each) and dug graves in the rocky ground for patients who didn't make it. Merrick and the doctor shared a bungalow, anchored by cables to rocks to keep the North Atlantic gales from blowing it away.

Sundays, fishermen would come up the hill for a prayer service that included favorite hymns, like "Throw out the Lifeline" and "Jesus, Savior, Pilot Me," and a short homily, normally delivered by Dr. Paddon. Once, when he was away, that duty fell to Wetherill. "He was so nervous, he got mixed," Merrick recalled, "and in an impassioned voice proclaimed, 'What did it matter if Jonah *did* swallow the whale?'"

At the end of the summer when the doctor returned to North West River, Merrick went with him as an unpaid teacher receiving only lodging and board. He spent the winter teaching Third and Fourth graders reading, writing, arithmetic, geography and carpentry skills. "They were lively, cooperative, charming kids," he recalled, "so glad to have books and stories and pictures that they could hardly contain themselves. After school, in the afternoon, we had to lock the door to keep them from coming back in again."

He stayed there the next summer—1930—as boss WOP with three Yale students. Most of their time was spent bringing in firewood to heat the hospital, school and dormitories in the winter. "We'd go up Grand Lake to where logs had been piled. The logs were six to twelve feet long. We'd throw them in the water, surround them with a boom and tow the boom home with a motor boat." Next day they would pile up the logs in big wigwam-shaped shocks, like ours at Cartwright.

"They expected a lot of WOPs," Merrick said. "There was a sort of British code that everyone should be *pukka sahib*—work without complaint, the stuff of generals. Grenfell came in every summer and exuded this British spirit. He'd dive overboard and swim to a growler, dance around on the growler and then swim back. He'd expect the WOPs to do the same. They weren't so keen on it. He was a product of the British Empire, but he inspired people to work themselves to skin and bone—a great leader."

The Labrador experience changed the course of Merrick's life. The lean, bearded volunteer married Paddon's nurse, Kate Austen, an Australian (the union produced three children and four grandchildren). He and his wife made the rugged September trek with North West River trappers by canoe and portage 350 miles up Grand (now Churchill) River into the mountains, returning with furs in January by snowshoe and toboggan. He captured the wilderness experience—its peace and rigors—in "True North," the first of his Labrador books. He taught English at two colleges, then edited a U.S. Forest Service publication for twenty-two years.

ANNE HOPKINS, who later added Burnham to her name, was a 20-year-old Vassar junior from Cleveland when she came across a month-old copy of the September 19, 1949 issue of *LIFE*. An article, "Labrador Mission," recounted a trip with Dr. Tony Paddon, Harry's son, on the *Maraval* down the northern Labrador coast that summer. With dramatic black-and-white pictures by George Silk, the text described the ship being pounded by a hundred-mile-an-hour hurricane, and Paddon and two shipmates setting out in a dory in the teeth of it to secure a line from ship to shore. The article told of the tuberculosis, scurvy and privations of the coast's people and the doctor's ministrations to them. It detailed a dog-team trip during which Tony Paddon had fallen into deep snow and, with a stick, barely fended off an attack by his huskies that could have killed him.

Tall, fair-haired, oval-faced Anne Hopkins had never heard of the Grenfell Mission until then. On the spot, she decided to offer her services at its Boston office as a volunteer. The choice meant rejecting a tempting alternative. She had finished second in a *Vogue* magazine essay contest, and the prize awaiting her was a year's employment in the magazine's New York office (first prize, a year in the Paris office, went to a young essayist named Jacqueline Bouvier).

The following spring the Grenfell organization notified Hopkins that she would be going to Spotted Island, at the point where the Labrador coast bends from north to northwest. There she would teach school, run a clothing exchange and cook and housekeep for a nurse and herself.

At St. Anthony she was given paper and pencils but no instructions on what or how to teach. She and an English nurse, Leslie Diack, were put aboard the *Maraval* with food for the summer and eight large barrels of donated clothing, some of it bearing nametags of the likes of Henry Cabot Lodge. Nurse Diack was to reopen the Spotted Island nursing station after a ten-year shutdown.

On the way north, the *Maraval* stopped at every hamlet so that Tony Paddon—as his father and Grenfell had done—could treat ailing fishermen and their families. He spent considerable added time helping them with government paper work or details of how to get their catches marketed. Once, when the surgeon was cutting tumors off the chest of a boy as he lay on the ship's dispensary table, the young WOP found herself in the role of operating room nurse, handing him scalpel, forceps, sponges.

Spotted Island, she noted in a journal illustrated with her own bright sketches, was a treeless expanse of rock and bog, inhabited in summertime by 105 people in twenty small frame houses. Among them there were only five surnames. She and the nurse shared living space in the dispensary building. They also shared the island's lone outhouse. She never did discover how the other islanders managed evacuations—probably by the dog "sewage works" of the Forsyth account.

As well as a nurse, the community had lacked a teacher for ten years, and Bill's Brook, the Spotted Islanders' winter home on the mainland, had no school. Reading and writing, therefore, were foreign territory to the twenty children, aged 5 to 16, whom their young instructor taught in the one-room schoolhouse. Laboriously, she set about drilling them on the ABCs, hampered by lack of a blackboard, any training on her part and considerable classroom disorder.

The teaching was subject to interruptions, once when Anne and the nurse went by boat to a nearby island to give inoculations, and again when a fisherman was sick and she filled in for him, helping to pull the net in a boat. "I got along very well with the people," she said. "I didn't feel like an outsider."

The summer had its raw moments. When a premature baby was born dead, Leslie Diack cremated the fetus in the dispensary stove, as her roommate cried out in shock. "Well," retorted the nurse, "what would you have me do with it?"

Afternoons in the schoolhouse, Hopkins spread out clothing on tables, arranging it by the size and sex of the prospective wearer, just as Macy's might. People would trade a sealskin, a loaf of bread or a jar of bakeapple (an amber ground berry) jam for garments. By the summer's end she had bartered away her whole stock.

The most harrowing event of her stay happened just outside the nursing station: a pack of snarling sled dogs set upon Charley Dyson, a tow-headed 3-year-old. Luckily, the attack occurred on a Sunday afternoon when men were standing around talking, not out in their boats fishing. They threw stones at the dogs to get them off the boy, who was covered with blood and screaming hysterically, but not before the huskies had ripped loose a six-square-inch section of his scalp. "We pushed it back on and bound it up, but we didn't sew it because we didn't know how," she said. When Dr. Forsyth at Cartwright would not or could not send a boat, Charley's father, Esau, took him there in his boat and the surgeon stitched up the wound. The islanders, under the Coast's immutable code, immediately killed all the dogs in the savaging, using a shotgun.

A week later she experienced a sequel of the incident. During a nighttime visit to the outhouse, she could hear dogs sniffing around outside. "I was scared," she said. "I stayed in the outhouse about half an hour and then ran like mad for the door of the house." When she returned to Spotted Island the next summer all the dogs had been isolated on a separate island.

In his autobiography, *Labrador Doctor*, Tony Paddon argued that carefully trained, properly fed dogs don't attack people. His own children, when they were toddlers, often played among his dogs and were never harmed, he wrote.

Returning after college graduation for the second summer, Anne Hopkins found her work a duplication of the first. At the end of it, however, she went to North West River where she had been asked to house-mother twenty-five schoolchildren in a dormitory. It made her workload at Spotted Island seem like a coffee break. With some help from a 17-year-old Inuit girl, she baked ten loaves of bread a night and cooked the kids' meals—the diet included fish, bread, canned goods, potatoes and apples. Every Saturday night, she heated water on the wood stove and bathed her charges, five to a tubful. Another weekly chore was washing twenty-five sets of clothes on a scrub board with a bar of homemade soap.

In November she was brought home by word of the desperate illness of her mother, who died of cancer a few months after she arrived. The Grenfell volunteer married Bradford Burnham, an industry executive, and was the mother of their five children, grandmother of nine and an accomplished artist. Before she died in 1993, they made their home in Hudson, Ohio.

She came away from Labrador much impressed with the work of the mission and its hospitals but disturbed by what she perceived as condescension of Labradorians by some mission people, including the Forsyths. That perception, however, definitely did not include Tony Paddon and his mother, she said. For several years back home in Cleveland she collected clothes and toys and sent them to the Spotted Islanders.

CYRUS R. VANCE spent the summer of 1936 in North West River and became intrigued by the people and the routines of their life.

Secretary of State in the Carter Administration, Vance was a 19-year-old out of Clarksburg, West Virginia, where his father was an insurance executive. He was about to enter sophomore year at Yale. With five others from the university—part of a total contingent of fifty WOPs that summer—he had gone up the coast on the *Maraval* which they boarded in Halifax. At North West River they lived in the school dormitory and performed the same firewood detail that had occupied Merrick: going upbay in a boat, encircling a flotilla of logs with a boom, towing them to the station, hauling the logs out of the water, stacking them in shocks and finally cutting them up with a power saw and stacking the lengths in a woodshed. Murdoch McLean and Ira Blake, mission employees, went with them on the wood-gathering excursions.

"It was a fascinating time," Vance recalled. "I liked the people we worked with, mostly Scottish, Irish and Indians... It was a small community, only a hundred and fifty or two hundred people. The Indians would come in the summer and camp on the delta." The village was host to two enterprises, frontier posts of the Hudson's Bay Company and Revillon Frères, competitors then for trade in what Vance calls "probably the finest mink in the world."

The rhythms of North West River life fascinated him. Village men, he learned, would go into the woods by canoe in

September to trap for furs (like Merrick's expedition). Beginning at age ten, their sons would be taken along to learn the ropes of trapping and surviving in the wilderness. They would come back out by snowshoe in December or January and return for another foray later in the winter. When a boy reached the age of 12 or 13, Vance said, he would be dropped off to work a "path" of traps on his own—a manhood initiation rite. His father would pick him up on his way back to town three or four months later. "It was sink or swim," he said. In late March and April the men and boys would go across Lake Melville into the Mealy Mountains to hunt for deer. Some of the venison they brought back would be eaten immediately, some put up in glass jars for winter supply.

The WOPs' work routines were interrupted occasionally by games and fishing expeditions. Vance, later captain of Yale's ice hockey team, recalled competitions that tested how many hundred-pound sacks of flour a contestant could carry over certain distances, a sport growing out of the trappers' upriver portages. They fished for sea trout with flies tied by Ira Blake with "good results."

His two months at the Grenfell mission, he said, "opened my mind to how much there was to do in different parts of the world to help those in need and to ameliorate diseases that had been brought in from the outside world."

A month before our conversation, Vance had told the Senate Foreign Relations Committee that the United States and its United Nations partners ought to press on with sanctions, diplomacy and a military presence, but not war, to achieve Iraq's withdrawal from Kuwait. "It was dead right," he said of his position. "Of course, when a decision has been made by Congress to go to war, you support the troops in the field. But it was the wrong decision."

A six-footer, dressed in a gray suit, striped blue shirt and figured blue tie, pink-faced, with eyes glancing keenly over his trademark half-glasses—Vance looked every inch of what he was: the presiding partner of a major New York law firm and a forceful player on the world stage. His life has combined private practice and public service. Among other roles, he has chaired three foundations, including the Rockefeller Foundation. Before his three years as Secretary of State (1977-80), he served as Deputy Secretary of Defense and Secretary of the Army. In 1991, at age 74, following routines that might have daunted someone half his age, Vance began serving as a United Nations mediator and peacemaker in places like the Yugoslavian states, Nagorno-Karabakh and South Africa.

In a four-decade career of public service, perhaps the most indelible memory he left the nation was his resignation as Secretary of State. It hinged on Carter's abortive attempt to rescue the American hostages in Iran in 1980. Vance was convinced the move was a grievous mistake with little chance of succeeding and likely to result in the hostages being shot by guards and in alienation of allies. When the "go" decision was made, Vance handed the President a letter of resignation. After the raid, which fell apart in the desert, the secretary followed through. "If you believe the President is making a mistake," he said, "you should be in a position to criticize [him]. It has to be a core issue; everyone gets overruled on some things. But if you don't stand up and be counted, it's unfair to the office and to the President." Such resignations occur in other countries, he said. "It should happen more here."

SHIRLEY SOULE SMITH was a summer WOP who ended up giving most of her life to the Grenfell organization. She was a year out of Wellesley and aged 22 when the mission posted her in the summer of 1923 to Square Islands, a summer fishing spot for livyers and visiting Newfoundlanders off the Labrador coast. "I was told to gather some kids and teach," she said. The Newfoundland government operated no schools in Labrador then. A couple of Protestant churches had volunteer teachers on Newfoundland's Northern Peninsula but none at Square Islands.

The "schoolmiss" rounded up more than a dozen children, ages 3 to 15, in the community's one-room schoolhouse. She began each morning with the song: "Did you start your day with brushing your teeth, Billy boy?" Then they got into printing letters of the alphabet and arithmetic. She read them stories.

Like a Peace Corps worker, she lived with a local family, that of John Campbell, a tall, white-bearded man who looked like a biblical prophet in knee-high rubber boots. Her room was reached by climbing a ladder through an opening in the living room ceiling. She ate the family's fare: fish, seal meat, duck eggs and chives grown in a local garden, washed down with tea and lime juice mixed with molasses. She paid for her travel expenses but not room and board; the Square Islanders footed her living costs in exchange for the teaching.

"The Campbells were superior people," she recalled. "I had a wonderful time. I wrote my family that I wanted to stay over the winter. But they said that wasn't wise, that I'd have to earn a living and I better get on with it."

The living she got on with was at the Grenfell Association's New England office in Boston. She worked there for thirty-five years doing public relations, raising money, writing letters and helping edit *Among the Deep Sea Fishers*. She gave me my WOP interview early in 1941 in Boston. A small, chipper, white-haired woman with a diamond-sharp memory at age 85, she was living in a compact bungalow in a big, inland development in Sunrise, Florida, when we talked almost fifty years later. The IGA had given her a modest pension.

She had a couple of disappointing visits back to the coast. The Campbells were gone; roads had been built; television's influence was flattening out the dialect. "It was too civilized," she said. She wouldn't go back again, fond though she was of

Labradorians. "They're uppity, proud. They're stubborn and individuals. I like them."

NELSON and **LAURANCE ROCKEFELLER** spent the summer of 1929 with Grenfell aboard his hospital ship *Maraval* as part of a crew of fourteen, including six WOPs. Nelson, a Dartmouth senior just turning 21, and Laurance, a 19-year-old sophomore at Princeton, were to perform assorted crew duties, with the older brother assigned as "official" photographer.

Their tasks had been worked out in an exchange of two letters from the missionary to the students' father, John D., Jr., and three letters back from him. "I have never lost any life when I have been aboard in all these 40 years," the doctor assured the father, a supporter of the mission, in a handwritten note.

The brothers' crew jobs, except for the picture taking, were upended early in the trip. The ship's volunteer cook was a Philadelphian with psychiatric problems whom Grenfell had accepted "to let him try and find himself again." They were hardly under way when he suffered an incapacitating "nervous breakdown," probably severe depression. The Rockefellers spent much of the rest of the cruise in the galley cooking, washing dishes and emptying garbage.

In another hand-written letter to their father late in the summer, the doctor told him, "Your boys spent infinitely more time in the galley than I care to think of... The boys did their job nobly and every member of the crew recognized it and was grateful..." This was Grenfell hyperbole to a doting parent. Elliott Merrick recalled that when the *Maraval* crew came ashore at Indian Harbor that summer, their general comment was, "We're starved. Nelson is the world's worst cook."

Looking for Laurance Rockefeller's office on the fifty-sixth floor of the RCA Building in New York, I stepped off the elevator and was faced with a bank of unmarked white doors. "It looks like a mail drop," joked William H. Whyte Jr., the urbanologist who worked with him for years. The hallway behind one of the doors leading to Rockefeller's office is dotted with pieces from his brother David's collection— African spears and wooden masks and antique Indian prints. Laurance's surprisingly small, sunlit office, cluttered with mementoes, was dominated by a four-foot gilt spread eagle on a wall.

He and Nelson, he recalled, loaded and unloaded cargo as well as doing K.P. that summer on the *Maraval.* "Nelson was bored," he said, "because he had so little to do. He thought the [mission] operation and the natives were very inefficient. I could type a little and I had a portable typewriter, so I was made a secretary to Grenfell. But I was very slow on the typewriter and Grenfell [who had a heart condition] would fall asleep in the middle of letters." Eleanor Wescott, the doctor's full-time secretary who was also aboard, said Laurance tried hard but his spelling was accident-prone: "Grenfell brought the letters back to me and every one had to be retyped."

They sailed as far north as Nain. Laurance Rockefeller, a tall, slightly stooped man with thinning gray hair and horn-rimmed glasses, got up and opened a panel on the wall revealing a dozen maps rolled up like window shades. He pulled down a National Geographic map of North America and pointed to Nain, two-thirds the way up the Labrador coast. Grenfell, he said, sometimes navigated by putting a Bible over the compass. "He was slowing up," he said, "but he showed spiritual strength."

Laurance's apparent appendicitis attack ended the brothers' summer on the coast in August.

After college, Laurance Rockefeller pursued careers in business, conservation and philanthropy. Nelson went on to become under secretary of Health, Education and Welfare, four-term governor of New York and vice president of the

United States for two years in the Ford administration. He died in 1979.

Tapping Nelson as expedition photographer proved to be inspired. He came away with 128 colored slides on glass, many of them good, clear action pictures. The Rockefeller name did not hurt in persuading Wide World to syndicate some of the photos. They were picked up and reprinted in newspaper rotogravure sections as far west as Cleveland and Chicago, netting Grenfell and his work a ream of good publicity.

JOSEPHINE COLGATE, of Morrisville, New Jersey, spent the summers of 1934 and '35 running a mission clothing store in St. Anthony and got some intimate glimpses of Grenfell. Mostly, these were favorable, but she was also seeing an aging man worn by his years. "He came into the clothing store," she wrote her parents, "and chatted with us for a while. He is a most charming and delightful man and so distinguished looking with his white hair and mustache. You can be at ease with him from the very first moment."

But soon she and her coworker Harriet Benson discovered cracks in the statue. They went to the Grenfells' for Sunday evening hymn singing. Everyone got to choose a hymn, and they wound up the singing with the Americans belting out "My Country 'tis of Thee" while the English joined in with "God Save the King." Then, she added in another of a series of long letters home, Grenfell "read a paper on crime in Chicago which was dull to say the least... One of Sir Wilfred's failings, I am told, is that he often misjudges his audiences, thinking they will be interested in whatever he is... He wanders from his point when he talks... another failing is he cannot remember faces."

They were invited back for dinner and a homey evening. After the meal they toasted marshmallows at the hearth and Grenfell read a few chapters of *Alice in Wonderland*, rereading it for the first time in many years, "and he enjoyed it immensely." Lady Grenfell, on the couch, was hemming dishtowels. "Their house is very ugly. It is called the Castle. The furniture is ugly and there is a lot of bricabrac and polar bear skins slung over chairs, but with it all it is very cheerful and home-like." Grenfell drew a picture for her and autographed one of his books "and I am very proud of it." She was swimming quite often in the frigid water, plunging in for an instant and then feeling exhilarated. "I am enjoying myself immensely. I like my work and the girls." Their diet included rabbit stew, cabbage, turnips, turnip tops from the mission garden and dandelion greens

Most of her work was selling donated clothes to local folks for small amounts or bartered goods to support the mission. Some of the contributed clothing was well beyond the pale: lounging pajamas, evening dresses, high-heeled shoes. Such stuff was dropped in the "make-over box" to be cut up and reworked into something usable.

She was invited to a local wedding at the Anglican church with a reception at the school where reels and sets were danced, a wholly new experience for her. "I've never known anything more fun or strenuous... the men are much more active than the girls. The louder they stamp and the higher they jump, the better dancers they are."

She and Hat Benson were asked to go on a medical run to Harbor Deep on the *Maraval* with Dr. Jack Steele. A couple of cases of diphtheria had been discovered and the provincial government asked the mission to immunize the town's children. After supper on board which the two volunteers prepared, Dr. Steele held a clinic in the ship dispensary with Colgate taking down names and diagnoses. An old woman came aboard saying she had "a wonderful bad ear" that she'd give $100 to get fixed. Dr. Steele examined the ear and said he thought he could fix it for $2.50 or a dozen eggs. He took her on deck with a syringe and warm water and squirted her ear for ten minutes. "Finally out came a lump of wax the size of a lima bean. He got one almost as big from the other ear. She was so grateful she could hardly talk. She said she could only afford ten cents. The last we saw her she was proudly showing the two pellets to friends."

Colgate had the salesperson's standard exasperation with some of the store's customers who "are not satisfied until they have seen almost everything in stock." But in one of her last letters she told of a group of women who walked seven miles from Goose Cove to St. Anthony, an annual pilgrimage timed for the opening of the store. They spend the night in St. Anthony and then shop early the next morning. "They consider the jaunt as quite a spree," she wrote, "even though they have to walk [the seven miles] in heavy rubber boots and carry all purchases back with them. It is really a pleasure to serve them."

DR. ROBERT B. SALTER, who became one of Canada's preeminent surgeons and an Officer of the Order of Canada, went to St. Anthony as a 20-year-old volunteer medical student in the summer of 1945 and repeated in the following summer. In July, 1948, a new-minted M.D., he married Robina McGee, a nurse he had met while interning at Toronto Western Hospital. They went directly back to St. Anthony for two years' work as all-but-volunteers: He was paid $1,000 a year, she $600. "Father carved and mother poured [ether]," said Salter of their surgical partnership.

As an unpaid medical student, he had taken patients' histories and done minor surgery on out-patients. As a doctor, he performed a full range of surgery and delivered babies. In his second year there, Dr. Curtis asked him to do all the hospital's operations. His most memorable case involved two boys with burns on 80 percent of their bodies. They had been playing with an oil drum, dropped a lighted match in it and overturned the drum, accidentally dousing themselves with flaming oil. With his wife acting as anesthetist, he saved them with multiple skin grafts.

"The medical community in St. John's resented the high level of medical care at St. Anthony before there was a medical school at St. John's," he said, sipping an iceless scotch-and-water and puffing on his briar pipe during a visit to Philadelphia. "We got some excellent doctors from the United States and Canada up there." At the University of Toronto medical school, where he was professor of orthopedic surgery, Salter established a scholarship for the senior student best exemplifying Grenfell's qualities of humanitarian concern.

Grenfell was gone when Salter came on the scene, but Curtis, who died in 1963, was a source of stories about the founder. A favorite, as Salter tells it: "On St. Patrick's Day Grenfell went to the Irish community of Conche—entirely Irish. He had gone to see a patient. The people were whooping it up. He wrote in his diary that he was disturbed to see a lot of people walking unsteadily. They must be suffering from beriberi, he wrote. He wasn't joking. He was not always a practical man."

Salter, senior orthopedic surgeon at Toronto's Hospital for Sick Children, served on the boards of the International Grenfell Association and the Canadian association. As such, he spent five or six summers on the Coast doing volunteer surgery and consulting. By then, St. Anthony was losing some of its rustic charm. When he was first there as a medical student, he recalled, there were only two motor vehicles in the village. One day, as if drawn by powerful magnets, they had a head-on collision.

HENRY CABOT LODGE, a U.S. senator from Massachusetts, ambassador to the United Nations and later to Vietnam and West Germany, was reared and groomed for public service. He began it in a modest way as a WOP. He and a Middlesex School friend, Edwin Merrill, were sent to St. Anthony in the summer of 1920. Lodge labored as a longshoreman, hauling supplies from ships, tarred roofs of new buildings and worked as a seaman on a mission ship. "He came back tanned and toughened," wrote his biographer, William J. Miller, ready for Harvard that fall.

He brought back from Newfoundland an odd bit of Grenfelliana. The doctor, he said, used to talk admiringly about a Christian Chinese general, Feng Yu-Hsiang, a convert to Methodism, who baptized his soldiers en masse by sprinkling them with a hose.

JOHN LOWELL came out of a Boston area family in which Grenfell service was as routine as brushing teeth. His father, Ralph, was the unpaid treasurer of the New England Grenfell Association in the 1930s. John was a WOP for two summers, in 1938 and 1939. Following in his father's footsteps, he served as treasurer of the NEGA for more than forty years. Three of his five children were Grenfell volunteers.

In both of his summers on the coast, John was one of nine deckhands on the *George B. Cluett*, the mission's supply ship, a converted Grand Banks schooner with an oil-fired auxiliary engine. At 19, he had graduated from Noble & Greenough School in Dedham, a Boston suburb, and was bound for Harvard that fall. He boarded the *Cluett* in Boston in June, 1938. They loaded on food and hospital supplies, plus oil drums lashed on the deck, and headed for Sydney, Nova Scotia, to take on coal for St. Anthony. The coal had to be shoveled into buckets in the hold.

They plied the northern Newfoundland and Labrador coasts, stopping at mission stations, with the WOPs unloading cargo. When they weren't stevedoring, they stood four-hour deck watches. "The work was rugged," he said. They slept in tiers of bunks in the fo'c's'le, "jammed in like sardines. The food was mostly cod or salmon and potatoes. If we ran short, we'd just jig for cod and go over to an iceberg and chip off a hunk of ice for the icebox to keep it fresh." They didn't work Sundays or at night. Evenings, they'd go ashore for mug-ups of tea and cookies with station nurses.

The ship, under both power and sail, was not deterred by fog and sometimes was steered by echo. Lowell remembers a near-collision with a merchant ship one foggy morning, and riding out a storm in the Strait of Belle Isle. "We had to heave to all night. We were very apprehensive about drifting icebergs that night."

John Lowell, tall and pink-faced, descended from a seventeenth century Newburyport settler, became a partner in a small trust company and an investment counselor. He and his wife, Eleanor, settled in Nahant on a finger of land in Massachusetts Bay. He headed both a local hospital board and the trustees of a college, and served on a settlement house board, in addition to his long service for the New England Grenfell Association. His work as a WOP reinforced in him "the notion of performing public service work for free," he said. "I've done that all my life."

9 The Three Colleagues

As for the WOPs, they were running the world as bank presidents, politicians, headmasters, head nurses, professors, physicians and surgeons and tending to the business of raising funds and recruiting staff.
Ronald G. Rompkey, Epilogue, *Grenfell of Labrador*.

Can an Episcopal priest-turned-social-worker, a car salesman, a psychiatrist and an ink-stained journalist run the world? Not unless a lot of people are looking the other way.

The Grenfell volunteer corps had its Vances and Rockefellers and Lodges. But for every chief there were scores of Indians like the four of us at Cartwright in 1941 who were lucky to be running our own bank accounts.

Two of that crew, Harry King and George Swift, were fortunate to make it out of their 20s; both had to survive ship sinkings. The one King went through changed the course of his life.

Henry Parsons King enlisted in the Navy in 1943 but wasn't accepted as an officer candidate because of an eyesight problem; "one eye sort of drifted off," said his younger brother, John.

On January 3, 1944 he was a 23-year-old quartermaster third class detailed to navigation on the *U.S.S. Turner*. The *Turner*, named for Captain Daniel Turner, a hero of the War of 1812, was a state-of-the-art Bristol Class two-stacker commissioned only eight months earlier. The 1,700-ton destroyer had just returned from an uneventful convoy run to Casablanca that had begun November 23. With other vessels of Task Force 64, the *Turner* was lying at anchor that morning two miles south of Rockaway Point at the southwest end of Long Island.

Before 6 a.m., before first light, King had gone to the messroom up forward for breakfast. There is no record of what the galley served that morning. By great good fortune, it did not appeal to many in the crew. They ate sparingly and left quickly, probably grousing about the creamed chipped beef on toast (universally despised) or whatever it was. The menu had the effect of clearing the area of many sailors.

As the young sailor sat there sipping his coffee, a voice spoke to him with urgent clarity. "Run!" the voice said. "If you have never believed in your heart, do it now!" The command was compelling. Leaving his coffee on the table, he got up immediately and walked rapidly aft to his living quarters. When he reached his bunk, he put on foul-weather gear—wind-blown rain mixed with snow was falling—and went topside. Just then, at 6:16 a.m., a shattering explosion ripped the vessel. "It sounded as if all [four] of the five-inch guns had been fired at once," he recalled.

The explosion's source was a magazine just below the messroom. Everyone in the area was killed. King concluded: "I was warned by God."

The blast destroyed the bridge, killing many of the officers, and flattened the mast, knocking out communications. It touched off an intense fire that overwhelmed all efforts to extinguish it. A New York pilot boat, first to reach the burning destroyer, plucked thirty-nine survivors from the water and sped them to a Staten Island hospital. The destroyer *Swasey* and other Task Force 64 ships closed in to offer help, along with a couple of Coast Guard cutters. Coast guardsmen lashed the bow of one of the cutters to the *Turner's* bow allowing the destroyer's crew to step across. King said he collected blankets to cover the injured. By then, the *Turner's* decks were hot from the raging fire. A Coast Guard officer told the crew to abandon ship. One hundred and ten survivors, some of them on stretchers, were saved by the cutter.

King said he was next-to-last to leave the *Turner*. Five minutes after they got clear, at 7:42, the main magazine blew in a thunderous eruption that shattered hundreds of plate glass and house windows in the Rockaways, Sheepshead Bay and the eastern shore of Staten Island. The *Turner* broke almost apart, rolled on her starboard side and began sinking stern-first in a haze of smoke and steam. The tip of the bow disappeared at 8:27.

The cause of the first explosion is still a mystery. The best guess is defective ammunition. Lost in the disaster were fifteen officers, including the captain, Commander Henry S. Wygant Jr., and one hundred and twenty-three men. Two officers and one hundred and sixty-five men were rescued. *The New York Times* the next day carried a picture of King and other survivors standing in the sick bay of the Sandy Hook Coast Guard station. He got out of it with nothing worse than a head cold. Credited with saving the lives of some of the burned and injured crewmen was the first recorded use of a helicopter in such an emergency. A Coast Guard chopper took two cases of plasma from Manhattan's southern tip to Sandy Hook, New Jersey, in fourteen minutes. From there the plasma was rushed to the Fort Hancock Station Hospital a mile away where many of the injured had been taken.

King told me his *Turner* story one clear spring day in 1981 as we sat in the lobby of a motel in Stowe, Vermont. Beefier than in 1941, with his familiar Kennedy-like Massachusetts accent and now with a cigarette habit, he was the same abrupt, opinionated, often enjoyable, sometimes difficult man we had known in Labrador. His transcendent breakfast message on the destroyer was off the record, he insisted. Asked why, he would give no reason. Lingering survivor's guilt, perhaps, or fear that a shipmate might rebuke him for not having shared his intimation. His death in 1983 mooted the directive. It turned out he had never even shared the experience with his brother.

After the war he returned to Harvard where he graduated in 1947. He enrolled in Episcopal Theological Seminary, as it was then called, in Cambridge, and received his divinity degree in 1950 but did not seek ordination on leaving ETS. Some psychotherapy sessions had led him to the discovery that "I was trying to repay God, and that is an unchristian reaction, since you can't repay God." He tried selling securities for a year (his father had been a stockbroker), but found that "my heart was not in it. The Holy Ghost was knocking at the door."

He accepted a ride with friends to San Francisco. Once there, he enrolled at the Church Divinity School of the Pacific, the Episcopal seminary in Berkeley, for a year's refresher course. When he completed it, he had no hesitancy in seeking ordination to the priesthood. "Nothing else made any sense," he said. "The therapy had been successful and I had found a calling, a true one. Salvation is free, and you don't deserve a nickel of it. You do what's good out of thanksgiving. We have a dour idea of all men, that sin is selfishness. The cure for it is the presence of God in our lives. It's like a small child crying because it can't have something. You pick it up and put it on your lap and it stops crying. Being on your lap is what stops it from crying. That's how the presence of God works."

After two years as a curate in a San Rafael church, he became a canon of Grace Cathedral in San Francisco where the controversial James A. Pike was Episcopal Bishop of California. "Less said about Pike the better," King said. The bishop later publicly expressed misgivings about Christian doctrines of the Virgin Birth and the Trinity, and finally renounced the church. As canon, King and another priest set up a downtown, working-hours chapel for runners, secretaries and other workers in the financial district. The chapel eventually was closed for lack of funding. "Harry was one of the kindest people I ever knew," said his brother, "but he was not a brilliant success in any endeavor." Chapters of his life kept coming apart.

Returning to Massachusetts, King was assigned by the Diocese of Massachusetts as vicar of two working-class missions about twenty-five miles north of Boston. After a few years there, he was called to be assistant rector at St. Paul's Church in Dedham, an upscale Boston suburb, but that ended after three years in a falling-out with the rector.

The most satisfying work of his life began with study during 1969 and '70 at Boston College that gave him a master's degree in social work. "There's a great need for counseling—for families and individuals," he said. "If a child is misbehaving in school, you look at the family. I thought I could be more useful doing that than parish ministry."

He went to work for the Catholic Charities Bureau in Salem as a social worker with a caseload and enjoyed it. But after three years that, too, fell apart. In 1975, when a heart attack at age 55 landed him in the hospital for six weeks, he retired to a red gabled, porch-girded, four-bedroom frame house he had bought in Manchester.

Its proximity to the home of his widowed mother, Mary King—within sight—was something of an irony. "It was not because he was [emotionally] close to Mother," John King said. "He didn't like our parents. He felt [he had been] pushed out. He felt unloved. They agreed to disagree."

Harry had been packed off to Groton as a seventh grader, an alarmingly vulnerable age for boarding school. Their father had been an athlete when young, first baseman on the Harvard baseball team and a hockey player. But Harry was "a little fat boy," said John. "He had two left feet," said his sister, Nancy. She was good at basketball, tennis and golf and their father's favorite; John, their mother's. "Harry was no one's favorite," his brother said.

Despite the *Turner* sinking—or perhaps because of it—Harry King was a life-long lover of the Navy. After finally getting his commission after the war, he served for 19 years as a naval reserve chaplain, rising in rank to lieutenant commander and going on regular summer training tours.

Grenfell had spoken twice at Groton in the 1930s, and King found him impressive. Eating lunch with Ruprecht in

Eliot House at Harvard, he heard about our planned trip to Labrador. "It seemed an interesting, cheerful expedition," he said. He applied to join us. At Cartwright he volunteered to stay over the winter, but Dr. Forsyth told him he was too young and unaccustomed to hardship for that. The mission experience taught him, King said, the importance of dealing with bodies, spirits and minds simultaneously. "Grenfell had to have schools," he said. "It was more than health. You can't convert a man who's hungry."

He never married. He wasn't gay, just not interested in marriage, his brother said. But family yearnings remained. A favorite epigram was: "Childless people need children." He had enjoyed taking some of his brother's five and sister's two offspring on trips to New Zealand, Australia, Tahiti, Alaska, Tokyo, Hong Kong and Bangkok. "He adored my kids," said John, "and the feeling was mutual."

The final phase of his life took an odd twist for a man of the cloth. He turned inward. He didn't get out much except to eat breakfasts at a nearby restaurant, his brother said. Paranoid about the possibility of an economic depression, he stocked his basement with case upon case of survival food. He invested in gold.

His death at age 62 followed a heart attack and a week in a coma.

My final recollection of him was at a dinner at a rustic but pricey restaurant in Stowe following our get-together. He had invited his niece, Claudia King, a nephew, David Putnam, and a few friends. The food was excellent; wine flowed freely. Harry was at his best, relaxed and buoyant, tossing off bon mots. As we chatted in the parking lot after the party broke up, he referred a couple of times to the adult Claudia and David as "the children." To them he was "Unc." The adult-child rapport he had missed with his parents seemed to have been established with the oncoming generation.

George Sedgwick Swift came out of a "Grenfell family." He met the missionary at the summer home of his Aunt Jessica near Grenfell's Kinloch House in Shelburne, Vermont. Jessica, a good friend of the doctor's, said he sometimes would get up in the middle of a dinner, leaving food on his plate, obsessed by memories of Labradorians with only tea and bread to eat.

Swift followed a family tradition of WOP service, a hard-luck tradition at that. The elder of his two brothers, Charlie, who was killed in World War II, also had been a volunteer at Cartwright. Chopping firewood with an ax, he had almost sliced off a foot. He was taken 200 miles by open boat to the hospital at St. Anthony where the foot was saved.

George Swift was four when his father died of Hodgkin's disease. Five years later his mother married Samuel Wagstaff, a New York lawyer, with whom George got along fine. They settled on Long Island.

Swift returned for his senior year at Pomfret after his Cartwright summer. Tall but skinny, he was light enough to be coxswain on the crew. After graduation and a session at a cram school, he passed entrance exams for the U.S. Naval Academy (Jimmy Carter was a classmate). Twenty-one months later, however, Swift flunked out. He signed on in the merchant marine and was assigned as a seaman to the Liberty ship, *William J. Palmer*.

On August 4, 1945, three months after the end of the war in Europe, the *Palmer* arrived at Trieste to deliver a cargo of horses and cotton to Marshal Tito's rebels in Yugoslavia. The British Navy had told the skipper the location of mines in the area. Even so, the ship plowed into one and sank in twenty minutes, just enough time to float some lifeboats and disembark the 30-man crew.

Back in New York, the 21-year-old seaman got a job delivering bills of lading on the docks. "But my nerves went to hell, and I had to get out of New York," he said. He and his mother and stepfather settled in Vergennes, Vermont, twenty-three miles south of Burlington. After some odd jobs, he began selling cars for the Vergennes Chevrolet dealer. That led to a sales job in the Chevy agency in Burlington where he worked for twenty years. Switching to the competition, Ford, he got caught in a layoff of older employees.

In 1981, when I first visited him, he was selling "reasonably priced used cars" for The Car Store in Burlington. The outfit's showpiece at the time was a green Fleetwood Brougham Cadillac with red leather upholstery which had been bought at auction. Its former owner claimed he had proof that the car had once belonged to Sophia Loren. Her mechanic must have lavished care on it. "It runs beautifully," Swift said.

When he moved to Vermont, he started attending St. Paul's Episcopal Church in Vergennes and became the church's organist and a lay reader. Even after he moved to Burlington he made the Sunday 46-mile round trip to St. Paul's, attending over a span of forty-three years.

He and his French-born wife, Renée, a former Montreal ballet teacher, live in a three-bedroom, white frame, brick-faced house in a middle-class development in South Burlington. Swift, his wavy hair, now silver, dressed in a blue blazer and gray flannels, with the same nervous laugh and friendly as ever, welcomed me at the door.

Renée Dumas, four years older than George, was the daughter of a French general. She and her first husband were members of the French Resistance during the war, blowing up trains at night, Swift said. They became parents of a son, Bernard, then divorced after the war. Trained as a child by a star of the Ballet Russe, she came to Montreal and set up a ballet school. Summers, she taught dance at a camp for girls on Lake Champlain where Swift met her. They married in 1960 and have no children, although Bernard, living in France and married with a couple of kids, is integrated into their family.

Like Harry King, Swift was now a smoker—unfiltered Pall Malls. "Less than a pack a day," he said in the tone of a man who has been asked before. As we gathered at the table for dinner. Swift's grace included mention of hungry people. Renée spread before us filet mignon with mushrooms and a lemon sauce, fresh green beans, freshly mashed and buttered potatoes, a mixed salad, cake and strawberries with cream, washed down with some French wine supplied by the guest. Julia Child could have done no better. After dinner, as Swift and I nursed snifters of cognac in the living room, Renée, once a student at the Paris Conservatory of Music and now a piano teacher, played Chopin and Schubert on her grand. With Edwardian grace she announced each selection before playing and acknowledged our applause with smiles.

When I returned almost ten years later, the Car Store had folded and Swift had retired briefly. He had gone back to work as a "greeter" in the used-car department of the Burlington Chevrolet agency. A greeter, he said, makes sure customers are waited on and "softens 'em up for the kill." He had worked there a couple of years before a stroke put him in the hospital for eleven days and ended his working life. As at the hospital in Cartwright, he got on famously with the nurses; they gave him a "diploma" when he left.

I expressed surprise at seeing him still smoking in the wake of his stroke. "Awfully hard to give them up," he said. "My doctor says he's more concerned about my drinking than the smoking... but I don't drink that much." He downed a couple of short highballs during our hour's chat. He had stopped attending St. Paul's in Vergennes because his coughing sometimes got so bad that he had to step outside. But his main health problem, he said, was his legs because he didn't get enough exercise.

Did so congenial a man miss daily contact with colleagues and customers? "Not at all," he said quickly. "I'm very happy to be retired, delighted to be able to sleep in in the mornings."

The 1941 summer in Labrador was a breakthrough for Archibald Lowell Ruprecht. Except for one brief stay at a summer camp, it was his first significant departure from home. He paid twice for leaving. First, with his father unemployed late in the Depression and the family surviving with the help of a benevolent uncle, the young traveler had to dig into his savings to help pay his way up the coast.

The other payment was in psychic coin. His mother, whom he described as a borderline psychotic, was fearful and protective to the point of smothering. Convinced that her son would be the victim of either a bear or a U-boat, she begged him not to go, then mortified him by going to the dean of Harvard College to seek help in having his trip canceled. As it developed, there was some U-boat danger: German subs that year sent five merchant vessels to the bottom within 100 miles of the Newfoundland coast. And a distracted black bear did turn up once near the hospital but fled back into the woods when people at the station came out to see it.

Dismissing his mother's fears, Ruprecht found the summer at Cartwright "mind-expanding—the first time I got away and had a successful experience." He also found encouragement for the medical career he was considering: "I saw Forsyth and Crenshaw in action and it gave me confidence in myself."

He had gone off to Harvard in 1939 and was one of several in his class who made the staff of *The Harvard Crimson*. He declared for medical school and was enrolled in the Army Specialized Training Program which took him through three years at the College of Physicians and Surgeons in New York.

He graduated but was not commissioned in the Army. At the end of senior year, a physical exam had revealed enough anxiety and depression to disqualify him for officer rank; he was placed briefly in a hospital psychiatric ward. A year's internship in three New York hospitals followed and then residencies in pathology, medicine and chest disease. Along the way he contracted tuberculosis which regressed spontaneously but was to surface later. While in New York, he embarked on the first of three psychoanalyses which would take a total of twelve years and cost tens of thousands of dollars.

He moved to Seattle in 1951 to become a staff physician at a chest disease sanitarium, still not confident enough in himself to launch out into the deeper water of private practice. Toward the end of the Korean War, however, his record as a physician led to a commission in the Navy. He spent two years treating families of personnel at the Seattle Naval Station.

A singular incident—a little like Harry King's on the destroyer—occurred early in 1956. The TB the young doctor had contracted earlier and which had regressed, flared up. He spent thirteen months in government hospitals getting cured. In the quiet of his hospital room one night he had what he calls a "white-light experience." It was powerful enough to get him out of bed and onto his knees. He heard no voice, but a strongly-felt "presence" communicated the message, "Follow me." "It made me almost glad to be sick," he said years later. "Someone, with a capital S, cared about me. I wondered briefly if I was nutty, but in the church it's known as grace. Nothing has been so tough since that year in the sack." Initially, he tended to discount the mystical command. Later, he began taking it seriously. Since then, "my life has gone more smoothly," he said.

When he left the hospital he was on the road to health, solid enough to embark on private practice as an internist. "I had had problems and went to others," he says. "Now I enjoyed people coming to me." He resumed the squash and tennis he had played as a boy, and made some real estate investments that went well. At the same time he became part-time medical director of the Seattle Alcoholism Treatment Clinic. During six years with the clinic he wrote a number of papers on alcoholism that garnered some national attention. Additional psychoanalysis moved him farther along the way. "It gave me the parenting I never had," he said.

At a "Junior Club" for young, single, college-educated people he met and dated Nancy, a saleswoman in a record shop. In 1962—he was 40, she 32—they married. The following year, a son, David, was born and two years later a daughter, Wendy. Like millions of other young families they moved to the suburbs for the schools, in this case across Lake Washington to Bellevue, and settled into a new house. After twelve years the marriage broke up. Five years later, now back in Seattle, he married again. But that union, too, dissolved. They separated in the fall of 1980 and were divorced the following year. "I don't believe I was blameless in either marriage," Ruprecht said.

In 1963, prompted by his own experiences in psychotherapy and a new interest in what makes people tick, he started a three-year residency in psychiatry at the University of Washington Hospitals. That led to private practice which continued until the breakup of his second marriage.

Recovery from a bout of depression in 1980 took seven months in a hospital, but it was his last detour on the journey toward health. As he ascended from the pit, he shed most of his private practice and took a two-thirds-time job with the Seattle Veterans Administration Hospital as admitting physician, dealing with questions of eligibility, transfers and cutting through red tape. He found the work satisfying.

What with illness and divorces, he had lost time with his kids. Once mended, he made up for some of it in trips with them, now adults. He and David did a tour of Europe that included visiting Ruprecht relatives in Bremen and Cologne and climbing in the Swiss Alps. A few years later they took in Japan. He and Wendy junketed around the British Isles and Paris, and in another summer basked in the midnight sun on a cruise to northern Norway, Spitsbergen, the Shetlands and the Orkneys—enlivening expeditions.

By the late 1990s, comfortably settled in a three-bedroom house on a hillside in the Wedgewood section of northern Seattle, he was still playing squash regularly.

For more than a decade he had been immersed in the life of St. Mark's Episcopal Cathedral parish, organizing weekend forums, writing essays for cathedral publications, taking Eucharist to shut-ins and leading its outreach to refugees from El Salvador. That effort included raising bail bonds and finding jobs and homes for members of refugee families the parish had taken under its wing. "I wanted to do more than just go to church," he said.

Wilfred Grenfell was a boyhood hero of Ruprecht's. He had read *Adrift on an Ice Pan* as a sixth-grader. It had stirred him, this tale of lonely survival in grim circumstances. The boy could relate to that kind of struggle. Grenfell might not have known where El Salvador was, but he likely would have cast an approving eye on one of his WOPs helping Salvadoran refugees find new life in an environment of opportunity.

10 Back North

Before I returned to Cartwright the first time in 1981 I had called someone in Newfoundland and discovered that something with the top-heavy name of Grenfell Regional Health Services was replacing the mission. Hardly surprising in the late 20th century that a 19th century construct like a mission would no longer be dispensing medical care in a nation as progressive as Canada. The only surprise was that it took that long to happen.

But what did that mean in Labrador? And what else had changed in the life of the people Grenfell came to serve? The only way to find out, of course, was to go back and see.

Cartwright turned out to be a likely vantage point for observation. Geographically isolated yet more and more connected to the larger world, with fewer than 700 residents it is a metropolis of the coast. Its isolation has had the effect of compressing change in time, making it all the more explosive when it came.

First, though, was the business of getting there. Forty years earlier we had gone by sleeper train to Sydney, ferry to Port aux Basques, coach train to St. John's and on the *Kyle* up the coast. I wanted to repeat those options if I could but time was limited: my paper, *The Evening Bulletin* in Philadelphia, which was to die the following January, had given me two weeks' unpaid leave to add to vacation. The coastal steamer was the essential leg for me but otherwise every day had to count. Thus, I booked a flight to Montreal.

As departure neared, however, the air traffic controllers were threatening their historic strike, eventually broken by President Reagan. With mixed feelings I scrubbed the flight and caught Amtrak's overnight *Montrealer* at 30th Street Station; it would take an extra day but it would repeat the original starting stanza.

Going by sleeper was to revisit forgotten delights: the lullaby of clicking wheels filtered through a pillow at night, the car's gentle motion, the exhilaration of waking to a new environment spinning past the window, in this case misty, birch-dotted woods. My last long train ride had been early in 1946 returning from the Pacific in the Marines. We made our toilsome way from Camp Pendleton through southern states to Camp LeJeune in North Carolina. The trip, interrupted periodically to replenish supplies, took five-or-so days but we were so glad to be back it didn't matter.

On the *Montrealer* some things had changed, of course. A tiny roomette had replaced the upper berth. The dining car breakfast no longer was served piece-by-piece on a white tablecloth. Orange juice, pancakes and sausage arrived on an airlines-type plastic tray, but it was hot and tasty, and service time was a fraction of the Pullmans'.

The train, an hour late out of Philadelphia, was delayed another hour when cars were added in New York to accommodate refugees from the airlines' mess. Then Canadian customs officers, checking passengers at the border, came upon a Greek couple who spoke no English or French. It was all Greek to the officers. Another hour elapsed straightening that out. Arrival at Montreal, thus, was more than three hours behind schedule. Flights to Halifax and St. John's were missed, and I arrived at my hotel after 10 p.m. sans luggage. Even so, I counted the rail trip a plus.

Leafing through the St. John's *Daily News* over breakfast the next morning, I was abruptly yanked back to Philadelphia. A picture taken in *The Bulletin's* newsroom, surmounted a caption reading, "Closure threatened." There was publisher Buddy Hayden talking to shirt-sleeved staffers, Stu Ditzen, Dave Kusheloff, Gene Herman and others looking glum as pallbearers. An article spelled out the bad news: if eight *Bulletin* unions did not agree to cuts of almost $5 million in annual payroll costs by August 16, the paper would fold, ending 134 years in the fabric of Philadelphia life and throwing 1,900 employees on the street. The paper's financial health was known to be fragile, but this call for radical surgery was stunning. To this former labor reporter, the chances of eight unions holding still for such a rollback seemed microscopic. If *The Bulletin's* obit was to be written in less than two weeks, then wandering employees should be back at work. I phoned Sib who had had a call from Pete Binzen, an old friend and colleague on the paper. Their collective advice was: continue the trip; time enough to return if the union deal fell through. With misgivings, I agreed.

Regatta Day in St. John's came up the following day. America has no equivalent of this sporting blowout. Cross Superbowl Sunday with the Fourth of July and put it all in one city and you approximate its local impact. Started in 1826, Regatta Day is the oldest continuous sporting event in North America. The day of rowing races celebrates the landing of Sir Humphrey Gilbert in St. John's harbor on August 5, 1583, taking possession of "New Found Land" in the name of Queen Elizabeth and launching Britain's overseas empire. On August 5, St. John's shuts down tight—public buildings, banks and stores close; only bars and restaurants stay open. What seems like the whole city repairs to the mile-long Quidi Vidi Lake in King George V Park at the east end of town to watch crews in six-oared, fixed-seat shells go at it. Admission is free. Between races spectators gamble on wheels of chance or throw rings to win teddy bears. Booths are sponsored by outfits like the Boy Scouts and the Lions. It is a decorous but spirited family outing, an evocation of an American county fair half a century earlier.

"Excitement at fever pitch for 1981 St. John's Regatta," read a *Daily News* banner that morning. Source of the ferment was word that, the week before, the Smith-Stockley crew had rowed the 2.4-kilometer course down the lake and back in nine minutes, twelve seconds. That unofficially broke a course record of 9:13.8 which had stood since 1901. *Eighty* years of improvements in equipment, training, diet—everything—and the record of those turn-of-the-century giants had hung there disdaining every assault. (The oldest modern track record, by contrast, Bob Beamon's 29-feet-2 in the long jump, stood for a mere twenty-three years before falling in 1991.) The Smith-Stockley rowers had been training all winter on a rowing machine and jogging long distances every day. With the official clock on them, could they repeat their warm-up performance? They could and did. In a light breeze beneath blue skies, with coxswain Jim Ring and most of the city yelling them on, they came home in 9:12.04, bettering the record by more than a second, winning the Lord Warden's gold medals and $1,500 in cash prizes put up by a trucking company and Friar Tuck's English Pub. It was a day of history for St. John's almost the equal of Sir Humphrey coming ashore.

Each Canadian province has a lieutenant governor who represents the King or Queen of the United Kingdom. The monarch is Canada's head of state even though the country became independent in 1931. In Newfoundland, a part of Canada only since 1949, the ties to the crown are probably stronger than in any other province. Head of state is not to be confused with head of government, the elected prime minister. The lieutenant (given the British "leftenant" pronunciation in Newfoundland) governor also represents the Governor General in Ottawa, the monarch's chief representative in the country. Less than a month earlier, Dr. William Anthony "Tony" Paddon, the Grenfell veteran from North West River, had been sworn in as lieutenant governor, the first from the Labrador part of the province.

Newfoundland, poorest of the ten provinces, is sometimes the butt of Canadians' "Newfie" jokes, and within the province, some Newfoundlanders have looked down on Labradorians as bumpkins. Mankind's search for targets of ridicule seems endless. Provincial services had been slow in reaching Labrador, too, a holdover from the conditions that Grenfell had found. Some northerners, bristling at their perceived status as second-class citizens, had responded by calling for secession from the province. Labradorians were even waving a homemade blue, green and white flag. Paddon had noted the disparity in a speech several years earlier when he and Dr. Gordon Thomas, IGA executive director, had received the prestigious Royal Bank Award. "Far more than salt water, the Strait of Belle Isle is also a barrier between two points of view, two standards of living and two attitudes," Paddon had said then. On the entire Labrador coast, he said, "there is not a single community water supply or safe method of sewage disposal... It is no argument that essential services are more expensive to provide in Labrador than on the island [Newfoundland]. If they are essential, they should be provided." Money was needed in Labrador, he said, "but even more, a sense of belonging, of being respected and of having a place in the province."

To be the first Labrador native tapped as lieutenant governor, therefore, was a double honor. The appointment paid tribute to Paddon personally and his thirty-four years' service with the Grenfell Mission. It also signified the respect for Labrador, the "sense of belonging" that he had been seeking.

Agreeing to an interview, he had invited me to lunch at Government House. The Georgian palace, 150 years old then, is a big, blocky gray stone building set on a hill in the capital and surrounded by a 12-foot dry moat. On its south side is a large greenhouse that produces flowers year-round. The mansion could be computed in multiples of twenty-two: It rests on twenty-two manicured acres, was staffed by twenty-two servants, and twenty-two are comfortably seated at its dining room table.

Paddon himself opens the door, slightly stooped at age 67, his gray hair receding from a tall forehead. This doctor, who once brought medical care a thousand miles at a clip by dog team through snow storms and bedded down on kitchen floors, is dressed in a black jacket and vest and striped diplomat's trousers, the uniform for a formal reception he had just attended. We pass a full-length portrait of Queen Elizabeth II in the hall and settle in a small sitting room where he pours sherry from a crystal decanter into crystal stem glasses.

Only that April the International Grenfell Association had willingly transferred health care services in northern Newfoundland and Labrador to the newly created provincial agency, Grenfell Regional Health Services. Grenfell had written in his autobiography, "All lines along which the Mission works should one day be self-eliminating," that day being when "this country is willing and able to take over the maintenance of the medical work." The day had arrived. Paddon discusses the transition at some length.

We move into the capacious, oak-paneled dining room and sit down at the end of a table almost as long as a bowling alley. The lunch—tomato juice, corned beef hash, tossed salad and a dessert of cantaloupe and grapes—is served on china marked "E II R" and lubricated with an excellent red wine. The lieutenant governor ruminates on changes on the coast. Diet has improved greatly, something both his father, Dr. Harry Paddon, and Grenfell stressed. The present generation, he says, is four inches taller than their grandparents. Tuberculosis was now "merely a nuisance"; when he began practicing, three percent of the fatalities were from TB. And obstetrical service has been so good that they haven't had a maternal death in seventy-five years, he says. When his brother Dick's late wife, Lydia, was visiting in North West River while pregnant, he adds, "I said to Dick, 'Why not let her deliver here? You've paid a thousand dollars for the delivery of each of your other children. You'll get this one for five dollars.' I think Lydia would have gone for it, but Dick wouldn't hear of it."

Grenfell, he says, was not much of a navigator ("he left red paint on half the rocks in Labrador") and not an outstanding surgeon ("he was doing so many other things"). "But he was way ahead of his time in seeing medicine as part of overall human biology, a great believer in preventive medicine, proper diet and exercise. He saw the necessity for education and cooperative stores. The merchants didn't want his co-ops competing with their stores. And they thought 'education would only make them discontent.' Well, I hope it would."

After lunch he conducts a tour of the mansion. Visiting members of the Royal Family are put up at Government House. The visits are not taken lightly: small golden plates on bedroom doors commemorate stays of individual royals. We wind up the tour on an ecological note. Paddon was about to visit Goose Bay at the invitation of NATO air force units there. Environmentalists, he says, had been fearful of the effect of military training flights on nearby caribou herds. Hunting caribou is banned, however, in a wide area around the airfield because of danger to the planes. "The caribou have discovered this and gravitate there," he says, smiling. "They seem to prefer the planes to bullets."

In 1941 the *Kyle* left from St. John's. Forty years later, the coastal steamer departed from Lewisporte, in the island-strewn Bay of Exploits on Newfoundland's northern shore. The bus ticket read Lewisporte but the bus didn't go there. Passengers were expected to know enough to get off at Notre Dame Junction, eight miles south of Lewisporte, and take a cab. The uninformed scrambled out the door just in time. Waiting at the dock in Lewisporte was the Canadian National Marine Motor Vessel *Taverner*, named for the captain who went down with the torpedoed *Caribou*. It is a 1,134-ton, 188-foot black and white ship with twin diesel engines capable of 2,200 horsepower—a little heavier but shorter than the *Kyle* and with the familiar foredeck crane. They don't need crewmen now to listen at the bow for echoes off bergs, however; radar gives them eyes. With a crew of twenty-eight, she can carry 102 passengers, although only twenty-seven were booked at the trip's start.

Shipboard travel is a sort of village afloat, a moving community far more than a plane, a bus or even a train. A ship provides freedom to move around, swap gossip with fellow passengers, get to know them and their concerns—like living on a street. And with this particular ship and its ports of call, there was almost no opportunity for dining or other entertainments ashore. This was no Caribbean cruise. The on-board community, therefore, was even more tightly bound together.

Cars could not be driven onto the *Taverner*, but a car could be carried on its deck. Shortly before departure, an orange Ford Fiesta was hoisted in a sling to the foredeck and secured by chains. Its owner, Nancy Breiden, attractive, blonde, newly out of Temple Law School in Philadelphia, and her friend, Steve Zwicky, a young Philadelphia lawyer, looked on. Having driven up from Port aux Basques, they planned to continue on from St. Anthony to the west coast of the northern peninsula and down that cliff-bordered highway.

At dinner in the dining salon that evening—shepherd's pie with mashed potatoes, peas and canned plums for dessert—a passenger asked a steward for a beer. No alcoholic beverages are served aboard, he replied, "because of the abuse of it." That, however, in no way meant that the ship was booze-free. A spirited party in the third mate's cabin, next to mine, started when we reached Triton around midnight and didn't end until departure at 3 a.m. The second night, when we put in at Harbor Deep, a hamlet on Orange Bay halfway up the northern peninsula and connected to no road, half a dozen boys came aboard. They looked barely out of puberty but were amply supplied with six-packs of beer. Fellow passengers, Bob and Inez, of Carbonear, Newfoundland, said their uproarious party ended only when the captain blew the all-ashore whistle at 3 a.m. even though the ship was staying in port until 6.

The *Taverner* seemed every bit as intimately personal a connection for people in the outports as the *Kyle* had been. Sometimes this ate into the timetable but it didn't seem to bother anyone. The second afternoon out of Lewisporte, for example, we made an unscheduled stop at Bear Cove, a tiny community on White Bay. The captain had been asked to pick up a parcel. Under a pale, watery sun we hove to three hundred yards off the mouth of the cove and loosed a whistle blast that echoed through the spruce-clad hills. Nothing happened. A man and a boy, fishing in an open boat off our bow, continued unperturbed. After about five minutes another toot signaled that we were about to leave. The fisherman, galvanized at last, started his outboard motor and foamed over to the ship. Told why we had stopped, he raced off to the cove. Fifteen minutes later he and the boy returned with a package the size of a standard typewriter wrapped in tan paper. Steward Bill Anderson lowered a hook on the end of a rope and hauled the package aboard hand over hand.

In the process, Anderson had noticed some fresh-caught cod in the bottom of the boat. He negotiated to buy the largest, a 20-pounder, for two dollars, ten cents a pound, and so fresh it was still twitching. He tossed the money down and pulled up the cod with the hook through its gill. When would we find fresh cod on the menu, I asked Anderson. Passengers wouldn't, he said; only the crew can eat fish not bought in a market. Next morning, though, as I was reading on an afterdeck, he delivered me a steaming bowl of cod chowder, dotted with bones and unchewable lumps of gristle but alive with North Atlantic flavor.

St. Anthony, a town of 3,100 people in 1981, is spread around a deep, protected harbor seventeen miles south of L'Anse aux Meadows, at the tip of Newfoundland's northern peninsula. The hub of that part of the world, the town then included a couple of motels with restaurants, two banks, churches, schools, a Hudson's Bay Company store (in 1981, just "The Bay"), a Sears and a self-serve laundry. Traffic on the main drag was heavy. Ubiquitous litter reminded this visitor of Philadelphia.

From earliest days, St. Anthony had been Grenfell Mission headquarters. The province may have taken over its work but the Grenfell presence still loomed. Foremost was the Charles S. Curtis Hospital, a hundred and fifty beds then but down to sixty-one by the century's end. It is a long, three-story, yellow brick building near the southeast end of town. Across West Street was a bronze statue of the missionary, parka-clad and toting a medical bag. Within view of the statue—a juxtaposition that might have dismayed the doctor—was a provincial liquor store selling spirits, wine and beer. It had not opened, however, until twenty-seven years after his death.

When the $3.2 million Grenfell Interpretation Center was opened in 1998 on the site, the statue was moved into an outdoor corner of the building. The center includes a state-of-the-art museum treatment of Grenfell and his mission.

Up the hill behind the hospital is the gabled, seven-bedroom, three-story, frame Grenfell House—The Castle—built in 1907, where the family, including wife, Anne, and their three children lived. In 1981, the Canadian and Newfoundland governments were sinking about $200,000 into renovating the house into a national historical site.

Up a steep, rocky path in back of the house, in a peaceful clearing of the spruce woods near the top of the hill, is a big outcropping of gray rock faced with six bronze plaques. In a recess behind one of them are the doctor's ashes. After a moment, a visitor familiar with Grenfell's story becomes aware of an odd omission. Etched in the weathered bronze are his full name, dates of birth and death and a favorite Grenfell aphorism, "Life is a field of honour." Nowhere on it or at the site, however, is there an indication—no small cross, say—to show that buried here are the mortal remains of a fervent Christian.

Dr. Peter J. Roberts, the transition executive director, was the last to hold that office with the International Grenfell Association, founded in 1914, and the first—since that April—in the province's GRHS. A rugged six-footer, he is comfortably dressed in corduroy trousers and an open cardigan sweater, a mop of dark brown hair falling across his forehead. A graduate of the University of New Brunswick where he also received a master's degree in history, Roberts earned his medical degree at Dalhousie University in Halifax. As a general practitioner, he worked for two years at the IGA's Roddickton station on the northern peninsula before coming to St. Anthony in 1975 to head the community medicine department. Four years later, when Gordon Thomas retired, he was named executive director. He is pleasant, candid, apparently a competent administrator, a philosopher in an antiheroic age. On the walls are sailboat pictures, reflecting a passionate Roberts pastime. The month before, he had turned 37 which is young to be the director of an organization of eight hundred employees scattered over almost 1,000 coastal miles, with a budget of $19 million. He comes from a prominent medical family; his father, Harry, a St. John's surgeon, headed the Canadian Medical Association; his brother, Edward, was formerly Newfoundland's health minister. "He's smart, clever," said a colleague. "And he's a Newfoundlander; this is the right time for a local person to be in that slot."

Before Newfoundland's confederation with Canada in 1949, Roberts said, most of the money for the IGA's work was privately donated. After 1949, the federal and provincial governments gradually took over financing. The day of the mission, in his view, had definitely passed. "The work has multiplied twentyfold," he said, tilting back in his desk chair. "Mission money couldn't have done that... This hasn't been a mission since the sixties. That's not the way you build a modern health service. People have a right to a service that goes beyond what a mission is willing to give them. The IGA functioned as a government when there wasn't a government [in Labrador and northern Newfoundland] and when people couldn't do for themselves. The IGA looked after welfare and education and medical care and jobs in industry. There was no suggestion that the IGA did not provide good work... but better ways were found to do these things—by government."

By the early 1960s, the Grenfell operation was down to health care and by 1975, he said, virtually all of its funding came from the national and provincial governments. In addition, the top of the association had lost touch. "The directors were former volunteers in their fifties and sixties who had had no association with the coast in twenty or thirty years, running a hospital they hadn't seen in years," Roberts said. The IGA brought in the American consulting firm, Arthur D. Little, to study the setup. "They said times have changed and so should the IGA," said Roberts. "So the IGA wasn't led kicking and screaming into the change; it was leading it."

Still, there were some who clearly would miss the Grenfell connection. While visiting the Grenfell gravesite, I had come upon Dr. Jenny Croft, a tall young English pathologist who had been in St. Anthony only a week. Before she left home, she said, some English nurses had told her they would think twice about working in Grenfell country now that the operation was no longer a mission. Nurse pay is lower than elsewhere in Canada, she said, and "they'll miss the Grenfell lure."

Bern Bromley, the rugged, red-bearded editor, publisher and prime reporter of *The Northern Pen*, in the weekly's jam-packed office, then in the basement of his St. Anthony home, had discussed the same problem. "Grenfell's crew were people who looked at coming to St. Anthony as a challenge," he said. "Now it's getting experience. A person wants to work to get some experience. He knows there's a cry for doctors and nurses. So they're here a few years and go someplace else. It has lost some of the respect it had in Thomas's and [former chief of staff Dr. John] Gray's day. It's more of a job now."

Roberts's response: "My theory is that here you can do good work. You have to have more commitment than a downtown nurse in, say, Philadelphia. But there's no religious aspect to it. The articles of association of the IGA said one of its purposes was extending the Kingdom of Christ. Governments are not in the business of that, and people are not interested in it, either. That age is gone. Even the Sisters of Mercy hospitals have a low religious presence. We don't attract hard-core missioners. If one is, then one goes to Bangladesh. But we do attract a lot of other people who aren't prepared to go to Bangladesh." As for pay, St. Anthony nurses in 1981 began at $15,000 and doctors at $39,000, he said. "That's not bad. Plus, they have perks—transportation up here, a generous pension, study leave. We assist in providing their housing."

The medical situation on the coast—he smiled—is now "depressingly ordinary." Until, recently, he said, "there were vitamin deficiency diseases, congenital diseases that you don't see now. TB in the '30s, '40s and '50s was a terrible problem. There is still TB in a couple of communities like Davis Inlet [halfway up the Labrador coast], but we pretty well have it under control." His staff sees a lot of trauma—industrial and fishing accidents. Liquor is a real problem, both in alcohol-related disease like cirrhosis of the liver and in violence and marital discord. "There's a high incidence of violent deaths, Skidoo accidents and exposure in winter," he said. The trauma, however, is not on a scale experienced at, for example, a downtown Washington hospital. "We're not killing each other yet. For a doctor trained to be pathology-oriented, that kind of hospital may be better—where a shooting victim is brought in every half hour. But it's not an ideal kind of society."

The child caseload was way down, too. In 1970 Curtis Hospital had fifty beds for pediatric patients. Now, only a decade later, they were frequently not keeping ten full. Why were children so much healthier now? "They live a lot better, eat better, live in better homes and are more aware of health," said Roberts. "There's better drinking water, better sewers and far better and earlier treatment."

Roberts, a general practitioner of community medicine, saw a paradox in preventive medicine, a subject close to his heart. He got up and paced to a window overlooking the harbor. "An orthopedic surgeon is not too attuned to preventive medicine," he said. "It's one of the biggest problems we faced: Traditional pathology-oriented doctors—if they don't find things to take care of, they feel short-changed. There's an absurdity here somewhere. We're supposed to keep people well. And if you do your job well, the demand for medical services is much reduced. But you find difficulty in recruiting doctors, who are juiced up for traditional work. The staff gradually shifts to community-oriented people who are comfortable dealing with the well. It's a return to the old aunt who used to keep people in the family healthy."

This was not reflected in any dearth of patients, however. Grenfell Regional Health Services treated 155,000 out-patients and 8,000 in-hospital the previous year, in addition to 20,000 with dental needs. In the opinion of some, like Dr. Donald Ainscow, an orthopedic surgeon from Southampton, England, too many people were coming to the health service with trifling complaints.

"Somebody ought to tell them that," said Ainscow, a tall, blond, muscular man, at Curtis for a month with his wife and kids to spell a surgeon on vacation. "They ought not to come in unless their ailment is preventing them from doing something important." Roberts's reply: "In England, Dr. Ainscow would be doing for 200,000 people instead of 40,000 here. His patients there would be far more serious. This is the nature of excess. We went from nothing to too much. It's difficult to justify it."

Even in St. Anthony, a coast metropolis, GRHS was a medical monopoly without competition by private doctors. If you got sick, you were brought to Curtis Hospital. If choice was limited, however, the rest of the deal might make saliva flow in the mouths of tens of millions of Americans. Admitted patients in 1981 paid a ward fee of $3 a day up to fifteen days, for a maximum of $45 (charges later abandoned). After that, nothing. The coverage is called Medicare and includes everybody. It doesn't pay for cosmetic surgery or unreferred second opinions. If a patient had to go to Montreal for treatment, Medicare would not always fund the transportation, Roberts said. Drugs were substantially covered. Patients at nursing stations paid nothing. And by professional standards—Dr. Ainscow's, for one—the medical care is good.

Patients rarely came to the hospital by boat now. GRHS had two air ambulances under lease and owned a third plane available for staff. If a nursing station could not treat a case, the patient was flown to Curtis.

The WOP program is history now. The system was a success in its era, Roberts said, but economic realities on the coast have changed. Now those tasks are done with government money, and it is partly a political matter. "You can't give jobs to volunteers if it knocks out a [paying] job," he said. "We might get back to volunteers if the economics are as uncertain as they look. We have a high standard of service. But it is expensive, and our society may say it's sorry but it can't afford this anymore." Four volunteers were working at the hospital at that time, doing portering work mostly. "But," he said quickly, "they don't interfere with paid jobs."

L'Anse aux Meadows, at the tip of the Northern Peninsula, has been a well-kept secret in the United States. Or was, anyway, until year 2000, its thousandth birthday, when a fleet of "Viking" ships and tourists from around the world were headed its way. "Beyond reasonable doubt," wrote historian Samuel Eliot Morison, it is the Vinland of Norse sagas, the place where Europeans—Leif Ericsson and some thirty-five comrades—first landed on this continent about the year 1000.

L'Anse is an easy trip from St. Anthony, less than thirty road miles north. At the site are reconstructed houses, their six-foot-thick walls of peat topped with grassy roofs of sod laid on wooden frames, and the foundation outlines of other houses. The Norse had eight in all, including a "great hall," 70-by-55 feet, a smithy with a stone anvil. And a sauna, their most glorious gift to the New World. Like all historic reconstructions, it is vastly neater and more manicured than the original must have been, corners squared, a woven sapling fence on the perimeter.

The name L'Anse aux Meadows is either a franglais term meaning bay of meadows, or as some believe, a corruption of L'Anse aux Meduses, bay of jellyfish. It looks northward past a rocky beach to shallow Epaves Bay. The settlement was discovered in 1960 by the Norwegian explorer Helge Ingstad after years of searching for Vinland. Ingstad had been working his way up the North American coast. When he reached St. Anthony, he met the mission's Dr. Thomas who invited him to join the hospital ship *Albert T. Gould* on a voyage up the coast.

"One day, after many disappointments," Ingstad wrote of that trip, "I asked yet another fisherman my routine question. He scratched the back of his head and said, 'Well, not so long ago George Decker over at L'Anse aux Meadows was talking about some ruins there.'" He went there and found Decker among the eleven fisherman families living in the isolated hamlet. Before him unfolded a scene that "dovetailed with the account of Leif Ericsson's arrival in the New World as narrated in the saga called the Flatey Book." (National Geographic Magazine, November 1964, p.727)

Three years of digging and dusting produced house foundations, a slate-lined fireplace, cooking pit, traces of a hearth, rusty nails made from smelted bog iron. Much of the findings resembled those of Greenland's Norse settlements; they were unlike ancient Indian and Eskimo villages. In 1978, UNESCO chose L'Anse aux Meadows as the first historic site to be placed on the agency's World Heritage List, ranking its preservation priority on a par with that of the later-added Pyramids of Egypt and Chartres Cathedral.

Why did Leif call it Vinland, or Wineland, since L'Anse is too far north for grape growing? One theory is that the sagas' word *vinber*, usually translated as grapes, really meant wineberry, which could be the area's plentiful wild "bakeapple" berries, currants or gooseberries. But Morison advances a more intriguing argument, that Leif was the hemisphere's first development promoter: "If it be objected that Leif Ericsson, after whooping it up at the court of King Olaf, must have known wine and would not have been put off by a poor substitute made from berries; one may reply that, just as [his] father Eric put the 'Green' in Greenland to attract settlers, so Leif put the 'Vin' in Vinland. And with such success as to throw off all Vinland seekers for centuries!"

The site, a national historic park since 1977, includes 19,906 acres and a visitor center. Peat for the house walls was dug seven miles away so as not to scar the park. The reconstructed buildings' six-foot peat walls sandwich a middle layer of gravel to drain moisture, just as Norse building plans from Greenland show. Pegs hold the wooden ceiling frame together, and skylight hatches are never closed. Not much rain comes in and they let in needed light. The hatches are also smoke portals. To reduce dampness, fires are lit regularly in the buildings, which are naturally warm in winter and cool in summer.

Wilfred Grenfell, as a private citizen, organized the first cooperative store in Labrador or northern Newfoundland in 1896, only four years after his first summer. It was at Red Bay on the southern Labrador coast, a village of twenty-five families among whom only one man could read and calculate. "Practically every family was then hungry," Grenfell recalled. The village staggered under debt, some of it inherited over generations, to a trader who kept accounts for the villagers. The doctor and the Red Bayers put together $85 in capital and set up a plan:

When the year's catch for the whole bay could be estimated, a schooner from the south would be summoned to take the fish to market. The ship's hire would be guaranteed by money loaned to the co-op. Since the schooner normally would come empty, it was arranged to have it loaded with supplies; revenue from their sale would pay for the purchase. The secretary of the store, the man who could read and figure, would go to St. John's with the schooner and "for the first time in history was to try to sell the fish for cash." The plan contemplated other savings: The middleman's profit would be eliminated; the fishermen would unload the supplies and load the fish, saving stevedore costs; fish salt would be imported at half the former credit price; the catch would be sold at a higher price than would ever have been realized from a middleman.

The scheme worked. By 1931, Grenfell said the store "had no debts, even in this depressed year, and had purchased all its supplies for cash and paid its shareholders a 5 percent dividend." The co-op had built a new store and had saved the village and the neighborhood, he said, while surrounding settlements had nearly expired because of the cost of living under the old regime. By 1931, eight co-ops were doing business in Labrador and the peninsula, including one in St. Anthony, "the biggest thing in its line on the coast," said Grenfell, where "the rule was cash for everything, even from members—no running up debt."

Fifty years later, in 1981, the Grenfell Memorial Consumers Cooperative in St. Anthony had long since severed connections with Grenfell except for the name. But it was still exerting influence. "If we ever closed," said Albert Sheppard, its unpaid president, "food prices in this town would go up 15 or 20 percent." A year earlier, the co-op had closed out dry goods and now sold food only. It was a basic medium-sized market with packaged goods and produce.

The store, with 700 members at $5 a share, had been through some tough times, "mostly a matter of poor management," said Sheppard, a balding, square-jawed man. "You can't stack the new stuff in front of the old... We had bills that weren't paid for two and three years. Checks bounced." Then they brought in a Canadian co-op society that took over management, although the nine-member co-op board still has control. "We've paid off the old accounts," said Sheppard, whose full-time paid job was assistant administrator of eight GRHS nursing stations. "We're not making money, but we're not losing any either." In 1999 the co-op was going strong. Its members, now numbering 1,000, were being asked to support a 50 percent expansion with the addition of a bakery and a deli and other consumer come-ons.

The last Grenfell enterprise still functioning as part of the IGA in 1981 was the handicraft shop in a white frame building just off St. Anthony's main street. By the end of the century the handicrafts were being retailed in a brightly lit shop in the Grenfell Interpretation Center.

What Grenfell called the "industrial department" had its start shortly after 1900 when the missionary, visiting livyers' homes, noticed mats that women had made of unraveled, home-dyed sacking material. These, he was sure, could be sold in cities to the south, bringing much needed supplementary income to fishermen's families. The doctor, an inveterate pen-and-ink sketcher, drew designs of sleds and dogs and icebergs for the women to copy and supplied them with materials.

He bought deerskins from Indians at summer encampments in Hamilton Inlet and gave them to fishermen's wives to be made into moccasins and gloves. He asked women in America, Canada and England to send their silk stockings to the mission to be made into hooked rugs: "When your stockings run, let them run to Labrador." The rugs are now high-priced antiques. In 1905 he met Jessie Luther who had started a handicrafts center in Marblehead, Massachusetts, for convalescing hospital patients, perhaps the nation's first organized handiwork therapy. Two years later he persuaded her to come to St. Anthony to organize the industrial department. In its heyday, the department was marketing the work of a couple of thousand coast cottagers in America, Canada and England.

Walking along West Street one day I had encountered Delrose Gordon, a nurse supervisor at Curtis Hospital. A Jamaican, she had gone to England in 1969 and worked in Wales, Kent and Guy's Hospital, London, before coming to St. Anthony. Everything about this petite, cafe-au-lait woman with straight dark hair was surprising, beginning with her presence in St. Anthony—like finding a quetzal in a henhouse. I asked where she lived and, as we were parting, was unexpectedly invited to see her apartment.

The living room/dining room of the apartment, in GRHS's Carlson House, gave a sweeping view of the bay. On the coffee table flew a small black, green and gold Jamaican flag. The apartment, including kitchen, bedroom and bathroom, came furnished except for a dining room table, so guests ate off lap trays. Rent then was about $190 a month. Nurses' salaries here were roughly the same as in London, she said, without disclosing hers.

How ya gonna keep 'em down in St. Anthony after they've seen Piccadilly? Well, she conceded, her new home was a bit dull by comparison, but in winter she had been playing badminton and volleyball in the high school gym and learning to play the piano. She had been told in London about the snow but arrived in St. Anthony in high heels. "The snow was up to here last winter," she said with an awed look, her hand four feet off the floor. She quickly bought boots. She had encountered no race problems here, she said, and she liked the rhythm of life. "You can do things at your own pace," she said. "In England, you run because everybody else is running."

My last night in town she invited me to dinner. The other guests—Kitty Prescott, a nurse from rural Saskatchewan, and Dr. Sam Mark, a resident surgeon and native of India—were there when I arrived. Delrose had the Canadian Open tennis matches on the TV and periodically let out a shout, "Well played!" making the place sound like an Oxford cricket pitch.

Dr. Mark, a short, black-haired, mustached man, told of getting seasick the day before when he had to go by small boat to a Soviet fish-factory ship out at sea. He took a crewmember with appendicitis back to the hospital. Mark, too, commended care quality at the hospital and called it a good place to work. Kitty Prescott remembered giving pennies to the Grenfell Mission when she was growing up in England. Like Jenny Croft, she believed that the end of the Grenfell Mission connection would dim the attraction of Newfoundland-Labrador service for English and Canadian nurses. "I came here to do my duty," she said with a lift of her head. It was the same lure that had led her to nurse work in Liberia. In fact, she thought St. Anthony's amenities would match Liberia's. Little envisioning the consumer delights of The Bay, she asked her daughter "to send me a care package with some toothpaste after a couple of months," she said, laughing. We feasted on poached salmon on rice, peas and carrots, potatoes, a mixed salad, ice cream and fruit cup, and the lap trays worked fine.

Next day began the trip's last leg aboard the *Petite Forte*, another CN Marine coastal ferry, bound for Cartwright.

Austin Curl is a modern Labradorian. Only a generation or so back, people of that rugged peninsula might have sailed widely on the offshore fishing grounds and made distant tracks by dog team in winter. But few ventured away from Labrador or knew much of the world beyond. Curl, then 31, his wife and two children and his father, Solomon, were passengers on the *Petite Forte*. They had been visiting friends in Carbonear on Newfoundland's Avalon Peninsula and were headed home to Petty Harbor, a southerly settlement on the Labrador coast. Having heard that I was from the Philadelphia area, Austin stopped me on the deck. The *Petite Forte*, a stubby, 173-foot black workhorse with a white superstructure, was rolling north past escarpments of battleship-gray rock and occasional icebergs.

He was curious, informed, opinionated. He asked about crime in Philadelphia and listened thoughtfully to my morbid account of murders, rapes and pillaging in the Cradle of Liberty. Television violence, he suggested, might be part of the problem. Perhaps, but Newfoundlanders, and now Labradorians, watch television, including some American programming. Why weren't they slaughtering each other at the same rate? Was it the tacit understanding that many Canadians seem to have that laws are to be obeyed? "Why do you allow so many handguns loose?" he asked. He would permit civilian access to pistols only at target ranges where they would be locked up when not in use. He conceded, though, that he owned a .22-caliber pistol that he used in hunting partridges and would not want to give it up.

Curl, mustached, brown-eyed, pink-cheeked, is a fisherman. So how was the fishing?—Labrador's perennial, number-one conversation topic. Poor this year, good last year, he said. Did the draggers (boats that pull a deep, wide-mouth net) overfish last year? He didn't think so. "My father remembers years when there were no draggers. Some years there would be no fish then, too." He did object, however, to their working Hamilton Bank off Labrador's Hamilton Inlet during spawning time. The coast's fishermen, he said, want dragging banned then.

Citizen Band radio has connected Labrador with places its residents hardly knew existed. While fishing, Curl communicated with home by CB, especially coming home in fog. In off-hours, he frequently picked up CBers from, of all places, Alabama. He had become friends, he said, of some of the Deep South "good buddies," and now was exchanging postcards with them.

Soon after we had left St. Anthony another passenger, a lean, black-haired man in a pork-pie beach hat, was criticizing the ship's accommodations to an acquaintance. "Terrible," he said, squinting at the moss-topped headland slipping past us in a steady rain. "I've seen women seventy and eighty years old sitting up all night." We were plowing north and west through the heavy swells of the Strait of Belle Isle toward Red Bay, our first port on the Labrador coast. This time there were no convoys to dodge. Nighttime bore out the passenger's complaint. The ship's smokeroom, now called the TV lounge, was two-thirds filled with sleepers, some of them past middle age. Two passengers bedded down in an outdoor passageway. Huddled under blankets, they looked like American street people.

Service on this ship seemed a cut below that of the *Taverner*. On the *Petite Forte* there was no towel in the cabin, no steward bringing drinking water, no paper towels in the public washroom. The door of the washroom would not stay shut against the ship's motion. Seated on the throne, one could suddenly be in view of strollers in the passageway.

My 9-by-5-foot cabin with double-decker metal bunks and a sink cost only $27 (Canadian) for the three nights from St. Anthony to Cartwright, a genuine bargain, I thought. But it stamped me as one of the privileged class aboard. Feeling guilty about the cabin's empty bunk, I offered it to Ed Bowdring who had given me a lift in his pickup to the dock at St. Anthony. With thanks, he declined and continued to sleep in a chair in the lounge.

The privileged, however, sometimes pay for their station. The first night when we tied up at Red Bay the steel roof of my cabin turned out to be the threshold of the gangway and a gathering place for beer-drinking, late-partying Red Bay teenagers. Was the contingent shod with wooden clogs? I could have sworn they were; their slightest shuffle on my roof turned the cabin into a tin drum.

Bowdring, a lean, bespectacled man with mustache and goatee, was filming under contract for the Canadian Broadcasting Corporation's *Land and Sea* nature show and was bound for the Black Tickle area to take footage of seals. He was a roving Good Samaritan. At Charlottetown, a hamlet just big enough to have a steamer dock, he and I debarked to stretch our legs. Women were loading boxes and suitcases onto a pickup. He started helping, prompting me to pitch in, too.

Farther up the coast he and others bore a hand in a small medical emergency. A stocky woman, gray-haired and in her sixties, slipped near the bottom of the main companionway and fell, banging her head into a bulkhead and leaving a two-foot trail of blood on the lower deck. Two stewards carried her to her bunk and started her recovery with first aid. The sight of her blood on the deck caused her teen-age granddaughter to faint at the head of the companionway and a younger grandson to go groggy. Bowdring led the boy to the dining salon and ordered him an apple juice which revived him. The granddaughter was brought around by a wet towel applied to her forehead by the Rev. Hugh Fudge, a priest in the Anglican Church of Canada.

Fudge was using the *Petite Forte* to circuit-ride some of the twenty communities in his 75-mile Parish of Battle Harbor. In summer he alternated travel by commercial plane, small boat and coastal steamer; in winter by Skidoo, everyone's generic term for snowmobile. He tried to touch each village in the parish twice a summer and once a winter. Most of the parish's residents, he said, are Anglicans, but the Pentecostals were moving in. The priest, 37, a native of Harbor Breton on Newfoundland's south coast, made his home with his wife and their 9-year-old son at Mary's Harbor.

Before ordination he had been a teacher at Cape St. Charles, farther down the Labrador coast, teaching grades one to eight, sometimes more than fifty kids at a time, all in one room. His chief problem then was boys in outlying fishing hamlets who started school late, in October, and left early, in May, to fish with their families. "They miss a lot of schooling," he said. Like everyone in Labrador, he paid close attention to the state of the fishery. Fishing was good last year, he said, but salt for curing much of the catch ran out. Six-foot stacks of white salt bags on every dock we visited evidenced a lesson learned. There was no dock at Snug Harbor where he left the ship. Dressed in a blue watch cap and black raincoat, he stood patiently in an open boat waiting to be taken ashore.

Soon after we left St. Anthony, I had encountered Solomon Curl, Austin's 76-year-old father, a cheerful, erect man in a gray felt hat and blue jacket. A lifelong fisherman, he had suffered two heart attacks. He was still keeping at it but in the light end of the work, "mending twine"—repairing nets. "I raised one of the largest families in Labrador," he said, "sixteen children." Of his twelve sons, one died of meningitis, one of a heart attack and one by drowning. Austin was the youngest of the surviving nine. We were passing the surf-girt cliffs of Quirpon Island off the northern tip of Newfoundland. It may have been John Cabot's first landfall in 1497 or perhaps even Leif Ericsson's 500-odd years earlier. Giving it my best high school French pronunciation—keerpohn—I asked Solomon Curl about the island. He didn't know what I was talking about. I pointed on a road map. "Oh," he said, "Carpoon. That's a French word."

Our conversation turned to Wilfred Grenfell. Sniping at Grenfell appeared to be in vogue among some writers in the province. It sounded like a mild form of colonial backlash. The missionary had brought enormous advances to the impoverished and neglected coastal people, but he was a child of the British Empire, sometimes autocratic and paternalistic. As the province matured politically, understandable resentment emerged about health care, now considered a right, being dispensed as charity. Some of that antipathy seemed focused on Grenfell. So I was curious about this 76-year-old patriarch-fisherman's opinion of the mission's founder.

It was brief and direct. "Grenfell was very well thought of," he said. "You see, before he came there was no doctor in Labrador."

The Curl family went ashore at Fox Harbor, about four miles south of their home at Petty Harbor. A veiled sun shone dimly through high clouds. Somebody met them at the dock in a pickup. Solomon was under orders not to lift anything because of his heart condition, so I lent a hand getting luggage off the ship and onto the truck. "When you came to Labrador," he sang out, easing into the truck's cab, "you never thought you'd get a job at Fox Harbor, did you?" "How much does it pay?" I asked as they moved off.

11 Medicine Minus Mission

Medical care in Cartwright had changed. Yet it was the same. Now the emphasis was on preventive care, better diet, less physician presence. But in 1981, at least, a doctor could still risk his life on a call just as Grenfell and the Paddons had done.

Dr. Peter Sarsfield was at his desk on the first floor of what used to be called the Lady Maclay Hospital and in 1981 carried the more pedestrian label of Cartwright Nursing Station (by the late '90s simply, Cartwright Clinic).

At 37, with thinning hair atop a tall forehead and an untrimmed brown beard, he bore a passing resemblance to the young Aleksandr Solzhenitsyn. The day outside was sunny and dry underfoot. But he was in his stocking feet, his shoes parked at the front door. The coast mandate, almost mosque-like in application—rain or shine, snow or dry—is that footgear is shed upon entering a home, and some public places as well, the nursing station being one of them. My wife considers the custom a cultural advance right up there with indoor plumbing. The debooting sometimes unveils surprises: a bald big toe here, a gaping heel there. In Sarsfield's case, the revelation was a dazzling pair of socks with inch-wide checks of kelly green, purple, canary yellow and magenta, knitted to order out of heavy wool by a yarn virtuoso named Lydia Poole in St. Lewis, down the coast.

More than the hospital had changed at the Cartwright station in the forty years since 1941. Lockwood School was unused and boarded up. The dormitory where we had stayed had been divided into small rooms and was housing workers who were bulldozing and blasting a pipeline and road up to a reservoir a mile back in the hills, replacing the one Pumphrey and his colleagues had installed fifty years earlier. By the end of the century the dorm had been leveled. A hundred yards across the road from the nursing station a two-story staff house had been built in the 1950s, painted the traditional white with forest-green trim.

Living in it were Sarsfield and his tall, attractive, dark-haired school-teacher wife, Rene (short for Irene) and their 3-year-old twin daughters, shy as fawns. Just off the road leading down to the wharf were the rusting remains of the little yellow Cletrac tractor the original pipeline crew had used. One immutable at what is still called "the mission" was the 60-yard, one-lane road that we had built behind the dorm out to a shed; it was weed-grown and uneven but free of potholes and holding up at least as well as I-95, granted with somewhat less traffic.

Dr. Sarsfield, the district medical officer, a tall, fast-talking native of Nova Scotia, graduated from Dalhousie University's medical school in 1973 (Peter Roberts's class). He spent three years working in North West River with Tony Paddon before coming to Cartwright in 1978. He called Paddon "a giant." The older doctor remembered his former assistant as "a very nice chap. He came in all fired up. He was a student in the 1960s. He always felt he was in a position of confrontation." If Roberts felt the mission's time had ended, Sarsfield was passionately convinced of it.

The idea of working for a medical mission may have drawn many to Labrador, but not the outspoken, pragmatic Peter Sarsfield. His work was virtually identical to what it had been under International Grenfell Association management, but he rejected the mission concept and deplored its impact on beneficiaries. "Working for Grenfell was no part of my motivation," he said as we chatted in his spare, unadorned office. "I stayed here in spite of Grenfell, not because of it. I don't like being identified with a mission."

Missionaries, he said, work hard and relish tough conditions, "and to that extent they're good. But there is a price to be extracted... We sowed the seeds of our own destruction. The missionary urge is to offer 'the truth' and to run people's lives for them. People have had enough of that. It was inevitable that they would... Twenty or thirty years ago people were very poor. The mission response was not only that they got [second-hand] clothes from Boston, they were told what to wear for work and what to wear for church."

"You extract subservience with a system like that," he said. "I stayed with a woman named Evelyn on the coast off and on for years. She had been educated at the [Grenfell school] at North West River. She was grateful for the education, but it had been drilled into her that the British way was right and the Labrador way was wrong. I remember attending a meeting with her where they were discussing things that she was eminently qualified to talk about. She said nothing because there were outsiders at the meeting."

The point was not new. In 1971 a St. John's *Evening Telegram* editor, writing ten years before the Grenfell Mission gave up the ghost, asked, "At what moment do the 'children' of a mission have the intelligence, wit and wherewithal to run their own lives without the paternal hand of the mission to guide them?... The most serious challenge faced by any missionary is not physical hardship or spiritual temptation; it is the intellectual sin which makes him feel that his work is never done. The very nature of his relations with the people he guides, heals or comforts makes him paternal, patronizing and superior... paternalism is a destructive force, for it makes people feel inferior... Wilfred Grenfell's children have grown up now and as adults should be able to go their own way."

Sarsfield was not so much stationed at Cartwright as functioning out of it. The previous year, he said, he saw 2,254 patients, traveling 156 days, or 43 percent of the time, more than half of it by plane or helicopter, 25 percent by boat and 20 percent by snowmobile. ("I record everything. You go to urinate, you record how much you pee.") He was responsible for eleven communities, from Paradise River, twenty miles up Sandwich Bay, to Mary's Harbor, 150 miles down the coast.

He visited each one every six to eight weeks. The following week he and his family were moving to a new assignment in North West River to escape so much time in the field. "Family-wise, it's a killer," he said, shaking his head.

Much of his focus, as Roberts had said, was on preventive medicine and education, less dramatic and often more frustrating than the curative side of the profession. In this part of the coast he had found "internal violence, not outward—ulcers and hypertension." The coast, Sarsfield said, had one of the highest rates of the latter in North America. It seemed anomalous that this urban malady, the bane of Madison Avenue ad merchants and stock exchange hustlers, should also beset isolated Labrador villagers. "There's so much salt beef, salt fish and salt pork," the doctor said. "We treat it with drugs and try to change behavior: cut salt in the diet, reduce stress, get exercise, cut the meat in the diet, cut the booze. Plus relaxation. But try selling yoga in Black Tickle." Food saltiness was to diminish by the end of the century as the Northern, the village's market, stocked fresh and frozen meats and fish.

Personal attitudes and habits—and government—were all part of the problem, as he saw it. "The major health problems are not malnutrition and infectious diseases that need a doctor. To get substantial improvement in health, communities will have to improve, to have a garbage dump, not toss it out the front door. [Weekly trash pickups fed Cartwright's dump.] We see people upset and anxious. They're trying to attain the urban dream in a remote place. One answer is to embrace wood heat. You have to exercise to get the wood and cut it, and there's plenty of it. But the Canadian government subsidizes oil heat here. Eastern Canada gets oil from the world market and the government sells it at less than cost."

Alison Howe, the station's brown-haired, apple-cheeked, 29-year-old public health nurse, from Durham in northern England, was trying to sell people on the virtues of wholewheat bread, just as Grenfell had. She found it uphill work.

"Brown bread is viewed as a sign of being poor," said Sarsfield.

Tobacco and alcohol were the coast's big substance-abuse problems, he said; kids as young as ten smoke cigarettes, some of them heavily. "People in their 40s come to us coughing and coughing with chest pains, a chest infection. Unless he quits smoking, he'll have ten more in ten years. People have to take responsibility for themselves." In southern Labrador, he added, alcohol abuse was less serious than up north in the Inuit communities. Here he found little violence or public drunkenness. "It comes in spurts, on a Saturday night or when people go up to Goose Bay," he said. Liquor and beer came in by ship and plane or was homemade of malt, sugar and vanilla. By the '90s beer could be bought at stores.

Some teeth were gnashed over dental care. "We get flak about the accessibility of dental service," the doctor said. In the station's basement are a dental chair and x-ray camera. A traveling dentist came to town six or seven times a year for up to a week per visit. Sarsfield was impatient with the flak. "We try to get the public to cut down on the amount of sugar in the diet," he said. "Some families I know in North West River let their kids have a Coke and a candy bar for breakfast, but they scream bloody murder if you don't have a dentist here all the time. It's a mission legacy—we will bring help, we will solve the problem, you don't have to do a thing." Eugene Hiscock, the region's representative in the provincial House of Assembly, said he encountered some of the same mind-set, "a tendency to look to this or that public agency or person to solve problems, not to themselves."

The emphasis may be on preventive medicine and the snowmobile had long since replaced the dog sled, but this is still Labrador. A traveling physician's practice had its tense, sometimes dangerous, moments, some of them even reminiscent of Grenfell on the ice pan.

Sarsfield remembered two winters earlier when he had scheduled a clinic at Black Tickle, sixty miles southeast on the coast. "I was going with a guide, an independent sort of guy," he said. Ignoring advice in Cartwright, including his wife's, against the trip, they took off in a heavy snowfall. "We passed Gladys Burdett's old house at Sandy Hill [roughly a half-way point] at noon," he said. "I was for staying there but [the guide] wouldn't hear of it. He's a kind of macho, nothing-stops-me guy. So we went on."

"We got lost," he said. "It started blowing about sixty miles an hour and snowing so hard you couldn't see your arm if you held it out. There was a lot of bad ice. After Sandy Hill, there was either bad ice or no ice." They were on two snowmobiles. The guide at one point had to circle around to find Sarsfield. "We couldn't see a thing. We decided we had to stop, so we got on land, but we had no shelter; there were no trees. This was about 2 p.m. We were soaked to the skin. It was mild, about 30 degrees, and the snow was wet. We tried to make a shelter behind the Skidoos. I was very cold. I crowded over against him for warmth. [The guide] went to sleep, but I couldn't get to sleep. If it had turned cold, we would have perished."

They finished the trip the next day and found that people at both ends of their route had been out looking for them, fearing that they had broken through the ice and were goners. As for the gung-ho guide, the doctor said, "I haven't traveled with him much since then."

That same winter he had experienced one of those round-the-clock, travel-and-treatment days that Labrador sometimes visits on its medicos. In rain during a January thaw, he had arrived, tired, by snowmobile at Port Hope Simpson from Mary's Harbor, twenty-five miles south. "I had finished supper," he recalled, "when we got a call from Fox Harbor. A man had a bad belly pain. It was raining and we had to go over some bad ice. I slipped through a couple of times into slush up to my knees."

"We went through one creek where the water went right over the Skidoo," he said gesturing with his hand, but it didn't stall. Fox Harbor is thirty miles around the coast, and four brothers of the sick man came to guide him, but "it took five hours to get there. We arrived at 5 a.m. The man was having a gall bladder attack. I gave him routine treatment."

While he was there he got an urgent call from Mary's Harbor to come quickly. "There was a woman in labor with twins. She was 40 and had had a number of children, and she was in trouble. The risks go way up at that age. She was in labor but not progressing." It was still raining, and he got someone to guide him back to Mary's Harbor, a three- or four-hour trip. "I got there to find two midwives and the woman in full labor with her cervix fully dilated which it had been for hours."

"The babies were not coming," he said. "They were locked inside. I tried to get a search-and-rescue plane. They couldn't or wouldn't come. The ambulance planes are single-engine and not allowed to fly on instruments. There was no airstrip [then] and no beacon lights at Mary's Harbor. We needed the search and rescue chopper which could have taken her to the hospital for a Caesarean section. We didn't have the anesthetic equipment there. We could lose the mother with a ruptured uterus and we could lose both babies.

"We phoned an obstetrician at North West River and he told us to destroy one of the babies, reach in and take its head off"—a classic abortion dilemma: whose life comes first? "Luckily," he said, "we didn't have to do that. One of the midwives asked her to do a very old-fashioned thing: get up and walk around. That worked. It dislodged the babies and she delivered. She named them Tina and Trina, one of them named after one of the midwives. I saw them recently. They're age two and fine, no sign of brain damage. The mother's fine, too."

Sarsfield felt he had something of the unhonored prophet's problem. "Last year," he said, "I was in Cartwright 147 days, and I was in Port Hope Simpson 35 days. In Port Hope Simpson, they say, 'Thanks, doc.' In Cartwright they want to know why I wasn't there all the time." The assumption was that the doctor can give better primary care than the nurse. "But I can't operate. I don't have general anesthesia. If I did surgery, it would be criminal, malpractice. We would lose a lot more—that's doctor talk for 'more patients would die'— than if we sent them up to North West River or St. Anthony. If I tried to take out an appendix after not practicing surgery regularly, too much could go wrong... Grenfell and Paddon and Gordon Thomas did well. But if we try to do what they did, we're not doing the right thing."

But suppose he had a case like George Swift on the *Kyle* and the ambulance plane was weathered in. What then? "That's happened five times in the last two years," he said. "There's a nonoperative way of treating appendicitis. You put the patient on IV, give him antibiotics, paralyze the bowel, give him nothing to eat or drink. You have to take it out later, but usually it heals up. There's more than one way to skin a cat." That particular skinning had worked in appendicitis cases he couldn't send out immediately, he said. "If it ruptures, peritonitis has to follow and if you have peritonitis you have a 50 percent chance of dying"—just the odds Swift had battled.

Jean Slimon, 37, a quiet-spoken native of Inverness-shire a hundred miles north of Edinburgh, was then Cartwright's head nurse. "The nurses are pros," says Sarsfield. "Jean is far superior to almost any GP [general practitioner] coming out of medical school. If I had to start a practice, she's a GP I'd love to depend on." The station was treating about 275 out-patients a month and fifty in-patients a year, plus ten or twelve a month sent on to the hospitals at St. Anthony, North West River or Goose Bay.

"Jean and Alison are the docs," Sarsfield continued. "They can diagnose and refer patients. If they want another opinion, they can refer to me. I'm a family-practice consultant." When he was in the field, the routine was for Sarsfield to call in to the radio-transmitter in the first-floor consulting room at 8.30 every morning. In addition, he said, "I make six to ten long-distance calls a day. Yesterday [looking in his record book] I made twenty." Is there a risk in Jean and Alison diagnosing? "There's a knack for them to tell me what I need to know and for me to know what to ask. It works well."

Like all systems, it occasionally came a cropper. A couple of winters earlier, Rich Martin, a 3-year-old Cartwright boy, had tripped on the raised metal edge of a living room carpet and fell, hurting his right thigh. One of his parents—Harry and Diane Martin—called the station and Jean Slimon came around to check out the injury. "She said it looked as though he had pulled a muscle," Diane Martin said. "It could have been bad. All the next day he was in punishment. The nurse asked if he could be sent to North West River Hospital, but the hospital plane wasn't coming, she said. So Harry took him up by Labrador Airways to Goose [Bay] to the hospital at North West River."

"They x-rayed him," she said, "and found the femur broken, put him in traction and sent him to [the hospital at] St. Anthony. He spent five weeks at St. Anthony all by himself. They didn't send the hospital plane to St. Anthony; Harry took him to St. Anthony. I'm a little bitter... We have a doctor here but he travels. I talked with them and they said a child that age usually doesn't fracture his leg. If we hadn't had the money to take him to the hospital, what would have happened? As it turned out, the leg did not begin to set out of place, but people have this worry. I've asked the nurse why no x-ray machine here... and she said if anyone is sick they'll get the 'mission' plane here in a few hours and get him out."

In their case the plane had to go north that day and couldn't come to Cartwright. They did meet Harry at the airport in Goose Bay with the ambulance. "The nurse [in Cartwright] let him stand on the hurt leg," she said. "Later she said she felt bad." Ultimately, the fracture was pinned.

Sarsfield, who was out of town at the time, commented: "When the leg wasn't weight-bearing, there wasn't pain. Normally, with a femur break, there's a lot of pain. These are the biggest muscles in the body and they pull on the fracture; sometimes they make the bone ends pull over each other. The symptoms didn't lead Jean to think the leg was fractured."

Cartwright didn't have x-ray—still didn't at the end of the century—surprising progress-in-reverse since it was part of the equipment in Forsyth's time. All the federal stations in the Arctic have x-ray. Five or ten times a year it would be very useful in Cartwright, Sarsfield said. "It's expensive and you have to know how to use it. And the union of technologists is saying they'll make trouble for us if we don't have their people running them, trouble in Goose Bay or St. Anthony. If they withdraw their people in those hospitals, we've got trouble."

As for the plane ambulance, he said, "we don't have a perfect service, but the air transportation is among the best of it—two ambulance planes at a cost of $400,000 for each plane. This is the only place in Canada that has air ambulances. Actually, they couldn't get in that day. I could have made the same mistake, but it was not gross neglect. I know both parents well. The general view is that we don't have an urban service. If we had urban options, we would have had an easier ride; we would have had x-ray, and they would have seen a doctor."

Sarsfield had been hearing two arguments, almost political in tone, against his working in the field. "The left-wing argument," he said, "is that the nurse-practitioners are better primary health care workers than MDs. I have to be careful not to come in here and try to make Jean a bedpan basher, not that I'd have much success at it if I tried. But the argument is: Leave them alone and let them do it. The right-wing argument is that the only ones who do a patient any good are the consultants [specialists], so get them to a hospital. GPs are viewed as garbage. Now, however, there is a new swing back to GPs; health [care] is being seen as more than dispensing medicine."

The right-wing argument, he growled, "is a crock of bullshit." As for the other one, "there is something to it... [but] the nurse-practitioner status is fragile... The nurses need support; there is a need for a chain of support. The nurses want and need added access to MDs, and the communities want it. It fits the public perception of adequate health care, too, that health care is a right not a privilege. Medicare specifies 'reasonable access to an MD.'" Technically, nurses are not allowed to prescribe an aspirin, he said. "We ignore that rule. The physicians' lobby wants to keep the nurse-practitioners that way. The way around it is: 'if no physician is available.'" Except for the excessive amount of traveling, he felt comfortable with his district's system. "I feel needed," he said.

Like Hogarth Forsyth before him, Peter Sarsfield was a trenchant observer of the Labrador scene. He and his wife and Alison Howe and I were sharing a mug-up of tea around the Sarsfield kitchen table. Outside, a cold fog had blown in off the Labrador Sea. The coast, he said, was in a transition phase. "TV has been here only three years. Black Tickle doesn't have TV or radio. [Television] means outside values, changing expectations. You need a wage economy to buy things [advertised on TV], and you have here a subsistence economy. Their parents felt it was fine if they weren't hungry. Now young people want $4,000 Skidoos, plus trips. There is an apparent loss of the old, land-based values. There is an unstable fishery and a government not encouraging the inshore fishery... There's an identity crisis."

He poured out another cup of hot water, giving his tea bag only a momentary dip, a switch from the Stygian brews of old. "Quite a few parents are not married," he said, "but they have stable relationships. By age fifteen, 90 percent of the kids are sexually active. They don't come to us for contraceptive methods, and their parents don't criticize them if they have a baby. They just bring up the child."

The letter of the law, he said, is that the medical staff were not supposed to give contraceptives to kids under sixteen without their parents' consent. "I do," he said. "Three of our eleven nurses [in his district] will not. But all the nurses will refer kids to me because they know I will. The pill is the contraceptive of choice up here. Now, we are not nonchalant about the pill. There are side effects. We give physical checkups. We see youngsters on the pill every month. But we have decided that the pill is less dangerous than an early pregnancy."

"There's nowhere to go," said Alison Howe, "no movies [in summer], no guidance from parents. They stay out as late as they want. [Parents are] generally permissive; they don't restrict them, give them pop and potato chips when they want it. You see little kids with their teeth falling out. The parents shrug and say, 'That's all she'll eat.' Parents often give nursing infants a bottle of tea—'baby's bottle of tea.'"

Both nurses found their work in Cartwright interesting, challenging and varied. "Nowhere else," said Slimon, "would we be allowed to put up an IV or suture or diagnose."

Both had found aspects of local life to enjoy. Howe believed "nothing is as beautiful as Labrador." Like John James Audubon, Jean Slimon had become a committed Labrador bird watcher.

Audubon, visiting the peninsula's southern coast in the summer of 1833, found flights of puffins, guillemots, gannets and cormorants as well as rarer pomarine jaegers, Hudson's Bay titmice and horned larks. He did seventeen drawings in five weeks. He encountered clouds of mosquitoes and "caribou flies" and also "butterflies flitting over snowbanks," all in a countryside at once "dreary, poor and inhospitable-looking" and "wonderfully grand, wild—aye, and terrific."

Slimon had spotted a northern yellow-shafted flicker, a red-breasted nuthatch, a black-bellied plover and a rarely-seen American kestrel, as well as the common snow buntings, trapped by local kids to add to springtime soup pots. The small ducks I had seen skimming the harbor, she told me, were dorkies.

The nurse-in-charge, pink-cheeked with graying hair, had been in Cartwright for seven years, on call days and every other night and every second weekend. She was headed home to Scotland at the end of September for seven months of paid leave. Her rate had been $17,000 a year, plus overtime beyond a 40-hour week and a set fee for solo night duty. The medical staff all were paying rent for their housing. She had heard it said in the village, "Jean has made her money, now she can go home." It rankled. "I didn't come here for the money," she said quietly in her soft Scottish burr. "I wanted to travel a bit and I had seen ads in a nursing publication, and my sister had worked in North West River as a housekeeper." She liked Cartwright but didn't know what she would do after the leave.

She, too, had had her memorable Cartwright moments. One began late in an October afternoon with a radio-transmitter call from the nurse at Paradise River that there had been a shooting accident and she had no equipment to deal with it. "The small boats had been pulled out of the water [to escape ice] and it was too dark, anyway, for one of them," she said. So she hired a longliner, about thirty feet long, but it had radar. "We left here at 8 p.m. In the middle of the bay, it broke down; the battery went dead. But they managed to get it started again. Then out of the darkness came a light. It was a speedboat. They had been expecting us. We transferred into the small boat and we arrived at about 10 p.m." Slimon and the Paradise River nurse got IV going.

The patient, a man, had been shot in the chest under the arm by a rifle bullet, she said, but there was no exit wound. His legs were paralyzed. The nurse had been in contact by RT with Peter Sarsfield who was in North West River. "We had a tube into the stomach and into the bladder in the event of any internal bleeding. Sarsfield had advised doing that. The ambulance plane was sent down from North West River, and at dawn it took the patient to the hospital at St. Anthony. There they found the bullet lodged in his spinal column. He had been getting into a boat holding a loaded rifle. He slipped and the gun fell from his hand. He recovered, but he was confined to a wheelchair."

No medical emergency in Cartwright and its environs is ever likely to equal the catastrophic Spanish influenza epidemic of 1918-19. The outbreak apparently started in the Inuit village of Okak, 340 miles up the coast from Cartwright. In a 1930 speech, Wilfred Grenfell said two men convalescing from the disease were among the crew of a supply ship when it made its annual stop at Okak. "The inquisitive natives swarmed aboard," he said. "In three weeks, the living had to give up trying to bury the dead. Out of 365 Eskimo, over 300 were dead, including all adult males... The flu made its way south along our coast."

The Rev. Henry Gordon, the Anglican pastor at Cartwright and a bona fide hero of the epidemic, recorded in his journal its scourge in Sandwich Bay. He had been on a boat trip around the bay, part of his far-flung parish, in late October. He returned to Cartwright at 10 a.m. on the 30th, mostly to put ashore Roly Bird, a young man from Dove Brook serving as crew who had come down with a high fever.

"I had a feeling that something was wrong ashore," he wrote. "There was not a sign of anyone about and an almost death-like stillness..." The epidemic, he discovered "had struck the settlement with the suddenness of a cyclone and almost the entire population was prostrate." Going along the path to the parsonage, he met a Hudson's Bay Company employee staggering as though drunk. From him he learned that the whole settlement was down with the illness. It had struck two days after the mail boat had left.

After dinner, he went on an inspection tour of the houses and was "simply appalled at what I found. Whole families lay inanimate on their kitchen floors, unable to even feed themselves or look after the fire... A bad headache and an utter exhaustion seemed to be the prevalent symptoms." Only four residents were well enough to care for the rest: Gordon; Hayward Parsons, the HBC agent; his wife, a trained nurse, and a man named Doan. Cartwright had no doctor then.

Gordon and Roly Bird, who had recovered under the care of Mrs. Parsons, set about fetching food and firewood for the stricken until the parson himself was felled. A few months earlier he had been sent to bed for three days with a mild case of flu which he believed had given him some immunity when the more virulent version struck him in November. When he recovered he was faced with digging graves and burying victims, including Sam Learning, his churchwarden. On the day he died, Learning asked for Holy Communion. "I will never forget that sacrament," wrote Gordon, "and whenever afterwards I perform the sacred service, I shall picture dear old Sam manfully trying to incline his aching head at the name of Jesus, just as he always did."

With the ground like granite from the cold and the number of bodies growing, alternatives to burial became necessary. Parsons, emptied an HBC building and converted it into a mortuary. "We sent word around to outlying communities," Gordon wrote, "to scaffold the dead well up in a tree where they would be well preserved by frost and safe from starving dogs."

On Nov. 21 came chilling news from North River, eight miles across the bay: "Will Learning from Indian Harbor... found the place in a terrible condition," wrote Gordon. "Out of twenty-one people, he found ten dead, two or three next-door to death and the rest too sick and dismayed to do a thing... In one house about half a mile from the rest, four out of the family of five were dead. The one remaining soul was the old mother of 72 years, Aunt Liz Williams, whose fight with death is one of the most heroic stories I have ever heard."

When she was found, she had been living all alone for nine days, since the last of her family had died. "All that time," Gordon wrote, "she had been without a fire (this in Labrador!) and practically without food. In the porch were two buckets of solid ice. From these she would chop fragments with an ax and thaw them out in a cup under her armpits. Outside were the starving dogs, tearing everything within reach of them and watching [for] the least chance of breaking into the house. She was now in one of the other houses and doing well."

Gordon and four other recovered men formed a relief expedition that set out from Cartwright immediately. They had to break through ice to reach the settlement, then dug a mass grave in a sandy spot, buried the now-stinking corpses and helped the living. They took Mrs. Williams back to Cartwright with them where she recovered.

In Mountaineer Cove, out of four families only three children in one house survived. The parson and a group with him found a family to take in the children. But what to do with the bodies? "It was decided," he wrote, "that the only thing to do was read the burial service and cremate the remains by setting fire to the shacks." Since most of the dog teams had been lost, Gordon decided to walk home the twenty miles to Cartwright on bay ice by bright moonlight that night. "It did me much good for I had much to think about."

Twelve of Cartwright's residents and sixty-nine of the three hundred in Sandwich Bay perished of the flu. Some fifty children in the Sandwich Bay area were orphaned, well beyond the capacity of the St. Anthony orphanage.

To care for them, Dr. Harry Paddon of North West River joined the Rev. Gordon in setting up a boarding school/orphanage at Muddy Bay, four miles southwest of Cartwright. The parson lined up a young woman, Clara Ashall from his home parish, St. Helen's in Sedgwick, Westmoreland, England, to come and be the school's principal. The move, he wrote, was "providentially inspired." Three years later, well into her work, the attractive Miss Ashall and Gordon got married.

Grenfell, earlier opposed to the boarding school plan, was later won over and made the school and its dorm part of the mission. The school burned down in 1928 and was replaced by the Lockwood School which opened in 1930 at the Cartwright station. Cartwright's provincial public school, which was started in 1968, succeeding Lockwood, is named the Henry Gordon Academy.

"I came to Labrador for superficial reasons," Peter Sarsfield said. We were again in his nursing station office. "In 1973 I had finished medical school and I was looking for a place that was fairly remote. I was brought up in a small town; I had had my fill of big-city medicine and big cities. I wanted a rural or remote place. I was thinking about an Indian or Inuit community. I asked Peter Roberts what he recommended, and he recommended that I write Tony Paddon and ask for a job. He did have a job, and I got hooked on Labrador. It came to be more home than Nova Scotia. We're Labradorians now. We're here to stay. Rene has taught here in Cartwright. I feel most at home." (By the end of the century, however, according to GRHS, he was out of Labrador and in Alberta.)

The following week I ran into the doctor in The Bay store. He was with two movers. His goods had been lifted that day onto the *Taverner* bound for Goose Bay and thence to North West River. He and Rene and their daughters were to follow close on.

12 Change

George Williams, the scion of the aftershave lotion family, started dropping in on Sandwich Bay in 1905 to fish in the Eagle River, then as now one of the world's great salmon thoroughfares. Aboard his well-stocked sailing yachts, he brought the bay its only tastes of big-time luxury. On one occasion that amounted to a utilities breakthrough for Cartwright.

He had befriended the Rev. Gordon, newly married and living with his bride in the parsonage. Arriving in the summer of 1923 on a new and larger schooner, *Norseman*, he brought the Gordons a movie projector, surely the only one on the Labrador coast, with some comic and travel films. More important, he gave them the means of running it, an electric generator.

By the following fall the parson had rigged his house with electric lights and connected them to the generator. A few minutes after they were turned on the first night, flooding the house with eye-blinking light, an urgent knock came at their door. A neighbor, breathless from rushing, held a bucket of water. He was ready, he said, to "put out the fire."

The village as a whole had to wait another 39 years, until 1962, for Newfoundland and Labrador Hydro to bring them electric power, according to Diane Martin. She was coordinator of the Eagle River Development Association in 1981 when we spoke. Nineteen sixty-two was virtually yesterday. Americans, recalling the early '60s, can remember how much they took electric power for granted.

Cartwright's kaleidoscopic rush continued five years later with amplitude modulation (AM) radio. "Radio was the biggest thing," said Gordon Wiggins, then the manager of Cartwright's Coast Guard station. "Before that," said the stocky, humorous Wiggins, puffing on a curve-stemmed pipe, "Cartwright was really isolated. You felt Goose Bay was a thousand miles away. The only way we got information was by short-wave radio. When we got radio you felt Goose Bay was on the other side of the hill." Or on the other side of the kitchen table. On an average morning, a listener could hear birthday greetings, wedding anniversary announcements and items like, "Mrs. Stillman, call Andrea today," or "For sale, one used electric stove in fair condition. Call..."

Television made its Cartwright debut only three years before my 1981 visit. It's an apples-and-oranges comparison, but by 1955, 63 percent of American households had TV sets. In Cartwright, 1981 was still too early for any clear reading of the tube's influence. I was lodged with Wesley and Charlotte Bird, then operating the village's motel-pro-tem in their canary-yellow four-bedroom bungalow in the west end of town. Everybody in the house gathered in the living room to watch the evening succession of American sitcom reruns like *All in the Family*, *Happy Days*, *Mork and Mindy*, *M*A*S*H*, and a Canadian entry, *The King of Kensington*. The United States' Saturday routine had become locked into the family's schedule, too: the three Bird children, Trudy, then 10, Darrell, 8, and Sharon, 4, arose late and watched cartoons all morning, even when fine weather beckoned outside. "It's good, watching television," said Charlotte, an instant convert to telly. "Something for them to do, right?" In pre-TV times, she said, "they'd be gone all over the place."

Even so, television seemed not yet to have leached playful invention of out the children. The Bird kids joined their neighbors in playing for hours in abandoned cars or boats hauled up on the shore. They lowered and raised old tires on ropes as if they were anchors and pushed each other in endless combinations on a nearby rusty, seatless swing set.

Even before unpacking at the Birds' I had called home to find out how the vote of *The Bulletin's* unions had gone. The labor miracle that no one had dared to expect had come off. Three days before my call the final union, the pressmen's, had ratified the agreement, giving the paper its reprieve from execution. Its time, though, would run out soon enough—the following January.

Astonished but vastly relieved, I settled in at the Birds' with three other boarders. Wes Bird, a lineman for Hydro, was on a job at Port Hope Simpson, leaving the enterprise in the hands of Charlotte, short, energetic, wren-like. It was a hardway hotel, though. Running potable water, brought to the mission station fifty years earlier by Pumphrey and his colleagues, still hadn't reached the rest of the village, even though the province was at work that summer on the new system.

At the Birds', running water came from a shallow, polluted well, usable only for toilet flushing. For drinking, cooking, bathing, clothes washing and even floor scrubbing, water was dipped from two 45-gallon steel drums outside the back door. For many Cartwrighters this meant three weekly baths in summer and one in winter, accomplished in the ancient manner: ladling water into a pot on the stove and, once warmed, thence into the bathtub. Never were there more than a few inches in the tub.

During the short summer the barrels were refilled at $4 a visit by the volunteer fire department truck, hauling water from a pond several miles to the east on Black Head. From November to June, when contents of the fire truck tank would freeze, most people got their water from Burdett's Brook where it emptied into the bay, just as those at the mission once had. That meant hauling a water barrel on a komatik hitched to a snowmobile across a mile of harbor ice. Sometimes the maneuver was more than routine.

The previous spring during something of a breakup, Wes Bird was heading across the harbor on a 12-horsepower snowmobile with Trudy and Darrell on the komatik when the motor stopped. On weak ice it is important to keep a snowmobile moving; once halted, it can sink. That now was threatening. The machine, frozen to a small ice pan, nosed up. Cautiously, Bird got off and disconnected the vehicle from the komatik, which seemed safe enough on a large "ballycatter" (pan), and went for help. The children, who were not frightened, stayed with the komatik. A group of people, with snowmobiles, gathered nearby on what solid ice there was. Bird got a rope from the nursing station and he and others pulled kids, snowmobile and komatik to safety. Charlotte had been watching the hour-long rescue from her living room window, not realizing that her family was its focus.

By 1991, all that was history. The province had run an 8-inch plastic water main into Cartwright from a dammed hilltop pond south of town. All of its 250 buildings, including the nursing station complex, were now receiving clear, lightly chlorinated, gravity-delivered water. "It's quite a thing," said Bill Elson, then Cartwright's mayor, in what for him was a burst of enthusiasm. There had been only one hitch: in the frigid winter of 1987 the pond had frozen eight to ten feet deep and stopped the flow, but that had been fixed in the interim.

The houses were also hooked up (all but sixty of them in low drainage areas) to a parallel sewage system. No one seemed greatly concerned that the sewage was piped untreated into the harbor. Newfoundland had been asked to install a treatment plant, said Charlotte Dyson, the terse, plump, cigarette-smoking town clerk, but had made no commitment.

By 1991 no one was taking in boarders. In another march into modernity, the village now had the Cartwright Hotel, three miles out of town on the road to the airstrip. Having flown up the coast, I needed a ride from the airstrip to the hotel. Taxi service is not available but it's not needed; Cartwrighters are accommodating about giving strangers lifts. Mine came from a telephone company man in a stretch pickup. The hostelry turned out to be a motel, a long one-story building with ten bedrooms and baths and a dining room. That evening I feasted on fresh sea trout, french fries and a crisp vegetables-and-lettuce salad, washed down with a bottle of Labatt's. It was a meal beyond expectations a decade earlier.

Fifty feet from the motel stood a sturdy wooden platform on which rested another item of future shock for an old Grenfellite: a helicopter. The chopper, rented from a Goose Bay outfit, was being used by a six-person Canadian team staying at the hotel. They were searching for titanium on the Wonderstrands, the 35-mile sand beach just up the coast that Leif Ericsson had noted on his way to L'Anse aux Meadows. A startling Labrador anomaly, it is as though the Creator, with sand left over from New Jersey, had given the stern rockbound coast a 10-league plaything.

I spent only one night at the hotel, comfortable as it was. The next day Leela Subramaniam, nurse in charge of the nursing station, generously offered me accommodations in the station's staff house, normally occupied by the public-health nurse, then vacationing in England. Rent-free, it was an unrefusable offer.

Subramaniam herself was an agent of change. Gone were the days of a Canadian or British doctor in residence at Cartwright. The nurse-in-charge was born of Indian parents in Malaysia. She had been trained as a nurse and midwife in England where she had worked for twelve years. By 1999, after a year's further training, she was a nurse-practitioner (at no higher salary). And the nursing station, now called Cartwright Clinic, was no longer part of Grenfell Regional Health Services. Along with most Labrador health facilities, it had been split off to form Health Labrador Corporation.

One rainy evening Woodrow (Woodie) Lethbridge, owner and proprietor of the hotel, stopped by and we had a mug-up of coffee at the kitchen table. My leaving the hotel for the staff house didn't miff him at all; logical choice to make, he said. Then 35, with dark hair and drooping mustache, he is five-foot-11 and built like a linebacker although he said he had never played football. Two weeks earlier he had quit cigarettes cold-turkey and had been going through "sheer hell," he said.

The soul of an enterprising entrepreneur, he is a sort of one-man chamber of commerce, promoting tourism, sport fishing, new industry like lumbering. He was a helicopter maintenance man in Goose Bay when he decided in 1985 that he would build the hotel. Three years later he bought the land—he wanted it half way between the airstrip and town—and opened in February 1989. His wife, Alice, mother of their two sons, supervises the kitchen and room service. By 1999, the hotel had a staff of 14, a major Cartwright employer.

He talked about his father, Ronald, a fisherman and trapper, a widower at 63 (in 1991) who moved to Cartwright from Paradise River downbay in 1969 to take a job as forest ranger. "A very independent man," said Woodie. For six weeks in the summer he lives in a little cabin at North River on Sandwich Bay's northern lip.

"He does everything for himself. He built himself an ice house. He cuts 150-pound chunks of ice in the winter and piles them in there so that in the summer he doesn't need to be running back to Cartwright all the time for crushed ice to keep fish he catches." If he needs an ax handle or almost anything else, he makes it himself. "He does things the way people did them fifty years ago." Or, for that matter, 150 years ago. This Emersonian self reliance enabled him to live comfortably on $7,000 or $8,000 a year, said his son.

The three generations of the Lethbridge family illustrated on a personal level the compressed nature of change in Cartwright, beginning with the size families from which they came. Ron was one of 21 children (all survived), the third of his father's twelve by his first wife, with nine more from his second, at a time in Labrador when family manpower was deemed essential to survival. But he fathered a mere four and Woodie only two.

One Sunday afternoon Woodie drove me over to his father's comfortable modern bungalow halfway up the village's hill from the harborfront. Ron was watching television and smoking a cigarette—predictably, a roll-your-own. Half bald with a gray handlebar mustache, he is a big, rangy man with a modest pot belly and large, muscular hands. He quit school after second grade at age eight to go to work chopping firewood and trapping. "I had to help," he said. "My youngest brother [Chesley] and sister got to Lockwood School. I had to earn money for their board. Forty dollars a year, I believe. A lot of money then."

For his first six or seven years on the trapping paths he accompanied his father, then his two older brothers, finally heading out on his own. He left home for good when he was twenty. "I've had an independent and interesting life," he said with a short laugh. "You learn survival."

The walls of the ice shed at his wharf at North River are a foot thick and packed with insulating sawdust and shavings. "Nothing could serve the purpose any better, sir, and very cheap materials," he said. "I pack fish in there a week, and they are as good as when they were caught." The sprinkling of "sirs" in his conversation, reminiscent of Dr. Johnson's, was a holdover from his early 19th century English ancestors, preserved like a frozen fish in the isolation of Paradise River.

We moved outside and across the yard to a work shed the size of a double garage. The only concessions to the late 20th century I saw were two power tools, a saw and a planer. From a bench he picked up a knife he had made with a three-inch blade as wide as a finger, epoxied at an angle to a wooden handle. This is Labrador's famous crooked knife, used as a draw knife in crafting snowshoes and countless other woodworks.

He reached down a pair of homemade bearpaw snowshoes from a rafter. Trappers, he said, prefer the bearpaw shape, a rounded diamond about two feet long and eighteen inches wide, to the longer, narrower variety pointed in the rear.

"You can turn around in the woods [on the bearpaws]," he said. "With the other kind you get hung up in the brush and trees." Because of the bearpaws' width, the snowshoer takes a longer step, swings his legs more and finds the going "not as tippy."

Lethbridge needs about six days to make a pair of snowshoes. He starts by putting together a frame in the form of a cross. Then he selects a "good stick of green birch" for the rim and beam. If it's not right, steaming may be required for bending. "You choose short stock, six, eight, ten feet," he said, "open grain with no knots."

Most Labrador trees, slow-growing because of the winters, produce hard wood. "You have to find a place where trees grow faster, otherwise the wood is too close-grained," he said. He looks for it at the head of the bay. He uses the crooked knife to "pare the butt of birch." The position of the beam near the snowshoe's toe is important, he said: too close to the front or too far back and it can pitch the wearer forward or backward. Snowshoe webs used to be made of caribou hide, but since the animals can no longer be hunted locally, he substitutes fishnet monofilm which does not stretch when wet as the hide does.

Does he make these trapper's necessities for sale? "I dislike the job of making snowshoes too much to make them for sale," he answered.

Nonetheless, he had been passing on his know-how to five Cartwright schoolboys, including Woodie's son, Perry. His grandson was "picking it up fast," despite his difficulty as a lefthander in managing a right-handed crooked knife. Except for himself, Lethbridge said, "not one man in Cartwright makes a pair of snowshoes. There's one fella in Paradise River makes a good pair. If somebody doesn't pick it up, sir, 'twill be a lost skill."

The first Lethbridge emigrating from England to Labrador was a tinsmith, and his descendant has preserved that aptitude, too. He held up a box-like galvanized sheet-steel stove, a little larger than a standard mailbox with a round metal chimney pipe in three sections going off at an angle. The chimney leaves the tent through an insulated roof hole. His canvas tents are also Lethbridge-made.

Out in the woods, he had four "tilts," the log mini-cabins Labrador trappers have built for centuries. But even in the depth of a northern winter, with six or seven feet of snow underfoot and night temperatures well below zero, he preferred a tent. He would light the stove, get the tent warm, stretch out on an old caribou hide and sleep with no blanket or sleeping bag covering him. "You sleep one and a half or two hours," he said. "Then you get chilly, fill up the stove and go back to sleep. It's the most comfortable way to sleep. If you sleep in a bag and [let the stove fire die] you wake up in the morning with the tent cold, and you're shivery and your clothes are wet and frozen. This way your clothes dry out." By 1999, at age 71, he was no longer making overnight trips on the trap line or spending winter nights in a tent. "That way of life is gone now," he said. "No money to be made." The exception was the market for marten fur, "if you can trap marten up in the trees."

We wandered around the shed inspecting other products of his hand. Leaning in a corner were a pair of heavy, 8-foot spruce oars, strategically balanced for the rower. Hanging from the rafters on ropes was a canoe, its frame and planking of fir, the lightest wood available, he said, covered with painted canvas. Near the canoe was what he called a "sleigh," a 6-by-1-foot toboggan of oak. He got the oak from a boat builder and steamed the front to bend it up. Loaded with gear and furs, it was towed behind his snowmobile.

A leather worker as well, he brought out a home-made sealskin lunch bag and a pair of deerskin boots. Finally, we came upon a couple of ax handles of stone-white birch, sculpted with the crooked knife as expertly as any hardware store product and sanded smooth. "They last two or three years," he said, "and save me more than $10 a handle."

If he lived in Japan, he might have been declared a national treasure and be supported by the state. In Canada, he is a local phenomenon.

Woodie Lethbridge and his brother, Ron Jr., are described by their father as "successful trappers; they know survival techniques." But they got out of trapping years ago, too busy with more modern matters. Ron Jr. is a pilot with a regional airline, licensed to fly fixed-wing planes and helicopters.

Woodie, besides the hotel, was also into sidelines in the summer of 1999: he was in a helicopter maintenance crew in northern Labrador not far from Nain for an outfit exploring for cobalt, working twenty days on, forty off. In addition, he was headed for northern Baffin Island to transport fuel by helicopter to another group working on a radar-warning network that replaced the Distant Early Warning (DEW) Line. All this was to help raise the $85,000-plus it would take to send his hefty younger son, Dwight, to Memorial University of Newfoundland (MUN) in St. John's. "I had to find extra income," he said.

He was also being warmed in 1999 by his hotel's best year, partly due to its contract to feed twenty members of a crew building a road from Cartwright to Paradise River. They were lodged in a trailer camp a quarter mile down the road to town but ate in the hotel dining room. Crew leaders were renting three rooms.

The Eagle's Nest Lounge, in a wing added to the dining room five years earlier, was another factor in the inn's prosperity—a jolting touch of Las Vegas in Labrador. The lounge offered a bar, five coin-operated video lotto machines, a pool table also brought to life by coins, and boards for the town's dart leagues to shoot at. "We had to have it to operate year-round," Lethbridge said. "It keeps the hotel alive."

Completing the Lethbridges' transition into the 21st century, Perry is being trained in electrical construction by deHaviland, the Ontario plane company that makes the Twin

Otter, plying the coast for Labrador Airways. Dwight plans to study business and information technology at the university.

For generations it was known as the fish plant, but it has gone through more transformations than a pair of butterflies—and almost as quickly. When I first went back to Cartwright in 1981 the plant was processing salt cod, basically the same system that was used by 16th century Grand Banks fishermen from Portugal. Gutted fish were delivered by collector boats to the plant where a header chopped off the head and a splitter took out the backbone. The fish was washed and taken to a salter who laid it out, flesh up, and salted it with a shovel. The fish were then stacked for two or three weeks to allow the salt to "strike," after which they were warehoused and sold, the main markets being Spain and Portugal.

The plant, then employing thirty-five men and women at $5 an hour, was regarded as a "throwback" by its operator, the Newfoundland Fishermen, Food and Allied Workers Union. In Cartwright it was also a saline irony. Only four miles to the southwest, at Muddy Bay, the idea of marketable quick-frozen food had been hatched in the inventive mind of Clarence "Bob" Birdseye.

Birdseye, who helped pay his way through college by selling frogs to a zoo for snake food, first arrived in Labrador in 1912 as a summer WOP on a Grenfell Mission ship. He returned in 1915 and took over an abandoned post of Revillon Frères, the fur merchant, at Muddy Bay to raise silver foxes. Selling furs in the United States, he made a killing and married his sweetheart, Eleanor Gannett. Local legend has it that he learned the quick-freeze process from Garland Lethbridge, of Paradise River, (who died in the 1918 flu epidemic). But the young fox breeder observed on his own that duck and caribou meat, flash-frozen in the frigid winter months retained much better flavor and texture than meats frozen more slowly in spring and fall.

When Eleanor returned to Muddy Bay in 1916 after giving birth to their son, Kellogg, in the United States, Birdseye ordered several barrels of cabbages from Newfoundland to balance their winter diet of fish, meat and bread. He kept the barrels indoors until the temperature outside hit ten below zero Fahrenheit, then immersed the heads in salt water and moved them outdoors. The submerged produce froze almost instantly. All winter, whenever the family wanted greens, Birdseye would hack a cabbage out of the ice and thaw it out. It tasted garden-fresh. Now he knew that quick-freezing worked for both meats and produce.

United States entry into World War I in 1917 brought the family home where Birdseye continued his experiments. He discovered that slow-freezing of foods separated liquids from solids, forming large sharp-pointed crystals that ruptured cell walls. "When slow-frozen... products are thawed," he wrote, "the moisture is not all reabsorbed, but much is lost before or during cooking and carries away with it a large proportion of the food value and flavor."

In freezing with "extreme rapidity, there is no time for the formation of large ice crystals and therefore no apparent damage to the cell structure. Thus, a quick-frozen product may be entirely fresh even though frozen as hard as marble." All that remained to bring off the biggest revolution in food processing since the can was the invention and patenting by Birdseye of fast-freeze equipment. By 1926 he had produced the first commercially practical freezer, fifty feet long, weighing twenty tons. Three years later he sold his patents and "Birds Eye" trademark to the Postum Company (later General Foods) for $22,750,000, then the largest sum ever paid for a food process. With some of the payoff he built himself a Georgian brick mansion in Gloucester, Massachusetts. By several yardsticks, he had come a long way from Muddy Bay.

The fish plant finally entered the Birdseye freeze era in 1985 by converting to frozen fish. By that time, a lot of the villagers had beaten them to it. In 1981, for example, Max and Shirley Mullins owned two freezers with a total cubic capacity of thirty-nine cubic feet. "Most people here buy food in bulk," said Max. "We go to Lewisporte and buy meat, a quarter side or a half side and they cut and package it." The Mullinses also froze local salmon, trout and berries.

By 1991 the factory was employing sixty-five workers, almost twice the number of a decade earlier. But at that point stocks of cod, which along with salmon had been a mainstay of Cartwright income, had been sorely depleted. The following year the government shut down commercial fishing for six years and then reopened it only on a very limited basis.

Hope dawned from another quadrant, however. A federal fisheries study showed a large crawl of snow crabs, if that's the collective term, just north of Cartwright on Hamilton Bank. In 1992 the province and the national government paid for yet another plant transformation, to freezing crabs. By the end of the century, more than fifty people were working on eleven boats in the crab fishery, maybe a third of the number of local people who once had gone after cod. But they were keeping 150 employees (including Charlotte Bird), earning $10 an hour, busy in the crab plant on two 8-hour shifts from mid-June to early October.

Each crab boat lays down five hundred pots in strings of fifty or so and brings up a string in one pull. The conical mesh pots are four feet in diameter and half that across the top. Baited with squid, herring or mackerel, they are checked every three or four days. Keeper crabs have to measure 3 5/8 inches across the shell, and they cannot be taken when shells are soft after molting. The meat is not up to par then. Boats are equipped with a device that tests the shell strength of claws. Joshua Burdett, the Canada Fisheries and Oceans officer in Cartwright, said the crab stock was holding up well.

"If we find soft shells, we move to another area," said Burdett. "It's a flat, muddy bottom and we can locate them by sonar. We've been fishing the area for a couple of years and we know it pretty well."

Snow crabs normally live on sandy or muddy bottoms at a depth of ten to a hundred fathoms in 30-40-degree (F.) water. They mate in late winter or spring in an act that sounds vaguely human. The male holds the female until she sheds her shell, then deposits sperm into a sac beneath her abdomen. What follows, however, is pure crab. Over several days the female lays as many as 150,000 eggs, deposited on hairy appendages under her abdomen. The eggs, carried to the following year, change from bright orange to purple or black. Newly hatched crab larvae rise to the surface, where they are prey for gulls, and go through three stages of development before settling back to the bottom. Feeding on soft-shell clams, bristleworms, small crustaceans and anything else that comes to claw, they take about six years to reach keeper size.

Half the plant's output was going to Japan and the rest to the United States in 1999. With crab bringing a high $1.61 a pound, the factory—and Cartwright—was having a good year.

Other more exotic fisheries were opening up, too. Four scuba divers with scoops were bringing up 10,000 pounds of sea urchins a day from the bottom of Sandwich Bay for the urchin roe market in Japan. The fishermen were getting only sixty cents a pound for the sea urchins but add-on costs were mind-boggling. The roe—it had to be refrigerated fresh at the crab plant, not frozen—was taken by fast ferry to Lewisporte and then flown to Japan with an arrival deadline of 72 hours.

The factory also was handling welk, another delicacy on Japanese shopping lists which was harvested from a two-square-mile bed ten miles from Cartwright, and shrimp, frozen and aimed at dinner plates in Scotland.

Maybe the biggest change in Sandwich Bay's way of life was in salmon fishing. From George Cartwright's time and back into the mists of prehistory, the area had floated on the backs of salmon. In 1981 the bay's total haul had been a robust 516,112 pounds. Ten years later Cartwright's sixty-five commercial licensed salmon fishermen had taken only 16,000 pounds, but that was because of ice.

The ice in 1991 was the worst anyone in the village could remember. From the air it looked as though someone had carelessly swept piles of huge white glass shards up against the shoreline, blocking harbor mouths. The ice was so unusual that it attracted much scientific inquiry, reported on in a book, *Riddle of the Ice*, by Myron Arms (Doubleday, New York, 1998). What may have happened is that the atmosphere, warmed by greenhouse gases, caused increased calving of Greenland icebergs. These floated south along Labrador's "Iceberg Alley" chilling surrounding water and contributing to an ice pan buildup along the coast. Since the ice off Sandwich Bay extended down twenty or thirty meters, it effectively locked out most of the salmon which normally swim no deeper than ten meters.

In 1999 there was no abnormal ice problem but also no commercial salmon fishing, only sport fishing. This caused a certain bitterness in the community. "Money is at the root of it," said Blair Gillis, the mustached manager of the Northern store, Cartwright's purveyor of food and general merchandise. "Business and private industry make more money [in sports fishing] than off the commercial fishery." Any number of sportsmen can buy licenses, $20 for a resident and $53 for a nonresident. Along Sandwich Bay rivers there are some fourteen salmon fishing lodges, including the Eagle Salmon Club, a private outfit for wealthy anglers. Supporting this complex is a whole sub-industry of planes and suppliers that also includes the Cartwright Hotel. The salmon run has been increasing in recent years and some believe it may be strong enough to support both kinds of fishermen.

Leslie Pardy, a wispy, soft-spoken Cartwrighter who was 76 when we spoke in 1999, was a commercial fisherman from an early age. He believes the moratorium was simply to "give more fishing to the sportsmen." The Canadian government had lowered the commercial fisherman's limit to an annual 600 pounds. "You couldn't live on that," he said. "They starved them out." The government then bought up commercial licenses.

When I first talked with him in 1981, Pardy was the maintenance man at the general store when its owner was the Hudson's Bay Company. But that didn't stop his fishing for salmon. "You'd go out at 3 or 4 in the morning and haul nets and get to work at 8 and work to 6, and then fish to 11 at night," he said. "I had eight kids. I had to work hard." But eighteen years later all that was history.

13 Anne

The apogee of St. Anthony's 1991 summer was a visit by Princess Anne, the Princess Royal, on July 3. A raw northeast wind straight off the ice jam had people blowing on their hands as they waited for her to show up.

The British monarch, of course, is head of state for all of Canada. But some provinces—Quebec, say—are notably slower to celebrate the Commonwealth link than others. Among the readiest to roll out the red carpet for royals is Newfoundland, and most especially for the Princess Royal who is Colonel-in-Chief of the Newfoundland Regiment. She was in the province to mark the 75th anniversary of the regiment's Battle of Beaumont Hamel in World War I.

At 7.30 a.m. on July 1, 1916, under grievously mistaken orders, the regiment burst "over the top" from their trenches and began to cross six hundred yards of no-man's land. With awful efficiency, German machine gunners and riflemen cut the Newfoundlanders to shreds, killing 272 of them and wounding more than 400. Nearly every family in the colony had a member who was a casualty. It was the worst military disaster in the island's history. Even today the memory is poignant. Each July 1, which is also Canada Day, communities parade and lay wreaths on memorials. The St. John's *Evening Telegram* ran a color picture of the Union Jack at half-mast on page one.

Princess Anne and her party arrive early in the afternoon in three government helicopters under a barred gray sky and the watchful eyes of dozens of Canadian Mounted Police. Some in St. John's have objected heatedly that the province, the poorest in Canada, has laid out $130,000 for the visit. The Mounties are taking no chances even though the St. Anthony crowd seems entirely friendly. The choppers land in the parking lot next to Curtis Hospital, churning up a brown cloud of grit.

Americans are used to visiting politicians and show-biz celebrities grinning broadly as they arrive at festivities. Not the princess's style at all, not that day at least. Dressed in a green topcoat, thin-soled flats and a scarf knotted around her head, she looks unhappy, perhaps chilled, as she debarks. She has earned a reputation for public service and caring work in the Third World. But other than that, no one would have confused her with Princess Diana.

Bern Bromley steps forward to greet her. The editor and publisher of *Northern Pen*, St. Anthony's weekly newspaper, the red-bearded Bromley is also the town's mayor. He wears the gold chain of office around his neck. The princess proceeds across West Street to a small park, then dominated by the bronze statue of Wilfred Grenfell. Lining a flagstone path to the statue are adults and kids, including uniformed Boy Scouts. She moves down the path, occasionally stopping to chat in a low voice with a scout. Her infrequent smiles, thin and cool as the blustery wind, do not appear to dim the enthusiasm of the couple of hundred monarchophiles, energized by the presence of an authentic royal.

After viewing the statue, she is guided to a table bearing cookies, cupcakes and beverages. She accepts and drinks a cup of tea. Then it's back across West Street to the hospital's rotunda entrance, where Dr. Roberts, formal in a dark suit and tie, takes her on a tour of the rotunda's ceramic murals.

The work of the Montreal artist, Jordi Bonet, in 1967, these are striking pieces of art, unexpected in a village of some 3,000. The eight mural panels, ten feet tall, lining the rotunda's walls depict Grenfell and his mission's work, fishermen and cod, hunting and trapping, and Indians and Inuit in representational and abstract images.

After a stop at Grenfell House, stocked with memorabilia of the missionary and his family, the princess and her group take off in another explosion of noise and dust.

The only physical reminder of the 75-minute visit that she leaves behind is her signature in Curtis's guestbook, a large scrolled "Anne."

14 Hub

Look at a *National Geographic* globe and you will find New York, London, Tokyo, Moscow. And Cartwright. Not every village of 630 souls gets that recognition. It must be admitted that the globe also will show you Hopedale and Nain farther up the Labrador coast, even more modest metropolises than Cartwright. The *Geographic*'s cartographers are clearly uncomfortable with bare coasts unadorned with names. The globe even shows Alert in northern Elesmere Island, less than five hundred miles from the North Pole, which probably has more polar bears than people.

But the fact is that in the whole 700-mile sweep of the Labrador coast, Cartwright, small as it is, is the most prominent settlement (Goose Bay, 130 miles down Hamilton Inlet, isn't coastal). From the start it has attracted visitors like a magnet collecting carpet tacks. At first it was a matter of its cosily sheltered harbor. That was what drew George Cartwright. But its central location is a factor on a coast not teeming with other towns. It was no accident that Cartwright in the mid-80s became the only waystop of the *Sir Robert Bond* on its route from Lewisporte to Goose Bay. The great advantage of the Bond—hawsered to the dock, it seemed to eclipse the whole community—was that passengers could drive their cars and trucks onto it. But Cartwright has benefited the Bond, too.

Over the years most of the visitors have been welcome, but there have been exceptions. One such was John Grimes and his crew who looked in on George Cartwright early one morning. In his journal entry for 27 July 1778, the major wrote that he was awakened at 1 a.m. by a loud rapping on his door. A body of armed men rushed in to announce that they were off the *Minerva*, a Boston privateer mounting 29-pounders, manned by 160 men and commanded by Grimes. The *Minerva* was probably one of the thousand privateers licensed by American colonial authorities to make up for lack of a navy.

Cartwright was "their prisoner," he was informed. Four of his servants, he reported, had "treacherously" told Grimes where he lived. Thirty-six of the Cartwright contingent were either impressed by Grimes or left voluntarily. He valued the goods taken from him at £70,000. But he persevered; the Sandwich Bay bounty was too appetizing. In a month and a half the next summer, to illustrate, he and his men took 12,396 salmon, sometimes at a rate of 1,000 a day.

By far the splashiest visitation to Cartwright came in 1933 when twenty-four Italian flying boats roared into the harbor. William Moores remembered their visit well when we spoke in 1981. Moores, resembling a thin Charles Coburn of the movies, was the retired Canadian Marconi agent in Cartwright and a sort of village patriarch. He and his wife lived in a two-story house, conspicuous in a town of bungalows, with a yard abloom with flower and vegetable beds, also highly unusual, and—unique—a 65-foot artesian well producing potable running water.

If the community had a patrician class, Moores was its leader. "He's of the old stiff-upper-lip British tradition," said Eugene Hiscock, then representing the village in the provincial assembly. In earlier years Moores had been the much-admired auctioneer/showman at Easter church sales. Arriving at his home, I routinely removed my shoes, only to find my host fully shod. In his hand was a violin on which he had been playing religious selections. His people had arrived in Newfoundland, he volunteered, in time to sign a 1709 proclamation to Queen Anne pledging that they would fight the French. He produced a signed photograph of Wilfred Grenfell whom he had known well, he said. He and his wife spent winters near Laredo, Texas.

The Italian expedition reminded Moores of Theodore Roosevelt's sending the sixteen battleships of the Great White

Fleet on their 1907-09 round-the-world cruise. The arrival of the Italian fliers—the most ambitious formation flight in the then-short history of aviation—generated international news stories datelined Cartwright. Benito Mussolini had dispatched the squadron to visit the "Century of Progress" World's Fair at Chicago in a frank advertisement of his regime. It was an innocent moment for the Italian Fascisti, two years before *Il Duce's* cynical invasion of Abyssinia (Ethiopia), followed by further brutalities and alliance with Hitler. In 1933 Italian fascism was being widely hailed for bringing order out of chaos in the country, building public works and—its cliché achievement—making the trains run on time.

The fliers, under General Italo Balbo, left Orbetello, seventy-five miles north of Rome, in twenty-five Savoia-Marchetti double-hulled flying boats—flying catamarans under a single wing surmounted by an engine with fore-and-aft propellers. One plane crashed at Amsterdam, the first stop, killing a crewman and injuring two others. The remaining twenty-four flew on to Londonderry, Ireland, and Reykjavik in Iceland. From there they took off on the most perilous leg of the journey: the 1,500-mile, 12 1/2-hour flight to Cartwright. Skirting Greenland's southern cape in dense, freezing fog, Balbo ordered his pilots to fly in close formation to allow exhaust heat to clear ice from the wings of following planes.

At 4.40 p.m. on July 13, "the first of the seaplanes of the Italian air armada appeared, tiny specks in the sky above a wooded hill beyond Cartwright," *The New York Times* reported. In a light westerly breeze under a gray sky, they swept down on the harbor in formations of three. "In as perfect order as a flock of geese," Grenfell said. The last of the twenty-four arrived at 6 o'clock. Greeting them was the white Italian supply steamer *Alicia* and a launch carrying "the [unidentified] commandant of the port."

In a later radio talk, Grenfell noted that the aviators "were received by a company of our orphans dressed in black shirts and carrying bundles of faggots [the fasces was Italian fascism's logo] in honor of the visiting Fascisti. Labrador is fast becoming the halfway house between America and Europe." The Italians and visiting newsmen were lodged in the Lockwood School dorm, for which they paid $800. The visitors also added one hundred feet of floats to the mission dock to help in the provisioning of their planes.

Eighteen hours after touching down, the flying boats thundered off Cartwright harbor. After stops at Shediac, New Brunswick, and Montreal, they set down on Lake Michigan before 100,000 cheering Chicagoans and fair goers. From Chicago, they flew to New York, landing on Jamaica Bay to a 19-gun salute and the applause of 75,000 onlookers. Their East Coast stay included a White House lunch with President Roosevelt, a New York ticker-tape parade and a Madison Square Garden reception.

On Sunday, 5,000 people packed into St. Patrick's Cathedral. As the Italians, in gold-braided white uniforms, marched up the aisle, "many hands went up in the fascist salute," The *Times* reported. (The saluters must have squirmed in recollection a few years later.)

The squadron did not return home via Cartwright but chose a warmer route—"much safer," said Balbo—via Shoal Harbor, Newfoundland, and the Azores.

The flying boats' exhaust had barely cleared out of Cartwright when the coast's hub was host later that day to even more famous guests: Colonel Charles A. Lindbergh and his wife, Anne. Predictably, international news coverage again followed. Lindbergh, six years after his historic flight to Paris, was a technical adviser to Pan American Airways. He had flown his red and black single-engine Lockheed Sirius seaplane north to survey America-to-Europe routes via Labrador, Greenland, Iceland and Ireland. Anne was copilot, navigator, radio operator, photographer and log keeper.

For the couple, the trip was part work, part adventure and, perhaps most important, escape from the lingering nightmare of the kidnap-murder of their first child, Charles Jr., the previous year and the massive intrusions on their privacy that followed.

As they approached Cartwright, Anne noted in her copious diary, "Across an inlet were several big wooden buildings, yellow [sic], well built, the Grenfell Mission. It seemed deliciously cool as we landed. The gently rolling hills, pine trees, rocky shore, gray water look exactly like all the Grenfell hooked rugs."

Fog and rain socked them in for a solid week. They bought Grenfell industrial goods and expressed much interest in the mission's work. One evening, Anne wrote, they shared a meal with WOPs in the Lockwood School dorm: "A huge dinner at the Mission: a long table lined with boys—American, English, Canadian, Newfoundland, and a few women... A lovely wood fire, the flower on the table, Labrador tea, big geranium plants in the windows. The boys seem very young..." She was no stranger to the Grenfell Mission; her brother, Dwight Morrow, had served as a WOP at St. Anthony in the summer of 1928.

Lindbergh wired congratulations to General Balbo on his "splendid flight" and added, "we are extremely sorry to have missed meeting you at Cartwright but we greatly enjoyed seeing your fellow officers on the Alice [sic]."

On July 21, a cloudless day, the Lindberghs took off for Frederikshab, Greenland, and the international spotlight turned away from Cartwright.

Cartwright, as noted, also drew Captain Elliott Roosevelt and his crew in 1941.

The biggest and longest visit to Cartwright began in 1951, lasted seventeen years and was for almost everyone concerned a happy experience. The U.S. Air Force, in a Cold War agreement with Canada, set up a radar base on Black Head, the 500-foot hill three miles northeast of town. With the 130-

man unit came jukeboxes, pinball machines and three clubs with bars.

"When they came here," said Malcolm Pardy, a Cartwrighter who worked on the base as a vehicle maintenance supervisor, "I thought, uh-oh, foreigners. I thought there would be fights. Not one! They'd come down to house parties in Cartwright and everything was fine. I never saw a man there I didn't get along with."

One plus for the village was that the Air Force hired on 35 local people. Another, said Gordon Wiggins, was entertainment. "You could go bowling up there and people from Cartwright could use the gym," he said. "The bad part was the availability of alcohol. It made a few alcoholics. The NCO's club was open every Saturday night for a party. I found them good fellows."

Charlotte Bird, then a student at the mission's Lockwood School, remembers "the Yanks on the base would send a bus for us. They had parties for us. Scatter-time, they would show us movies like *Snow White and the Seven Dwarfs*. At Christmastime they would have a Santa Claus who would give each child a present according to his age. We looked forward to that." Before the bus took them back to the dorm, "the Yanks would help us put on our boots. Nice people."

The airmen pulled out in 1968 leaving behind four 40-foot gray radar screen saucers and a hamlet of buildings. One day in 1981, with a west wind pushing low clouds across the top of Black Head, I walked up to look at what was left of the base. The climb was invigorating but not the sight at the hilltop. The buildings had been ripped apart by people searching for lumber—anything of value—leaving behind a shambles. A tornado couldn't have wrecked it worse. This American winced in shame to see a U.S. base left in such a mess. By 1991, the Canadian government, doing what their guests had left undone, had cleaned it up.

15 Road

Cartwright has been connected to the wider world by sea-lanes forever. Coastal ferries, descendants of the *Kyle*, with their milk-run routes, still stop at the village. And, of course, since the mid-80s, so does the coastal liner *Sir Robert Bond*. Evolution had also touched air travel to Cartwright. In 1981 when the airstrip was half-built, Air Labrador's floatplanes landed in the harbor just like Lindbergh's. Ten years later the Twin Otters were using the completed strip. On the drawing board in 1999 was a plan to expand the field to accommodate larger, 35-passenger planes.

But never had there been a road into the village. The closest inter-town highway was 135 miles away. This, as you can imagine, had impacted the village's way of life. Many car and pickup owners, for instance, left keys in their ignitions. Nobody stole cars; where could you take them?

The big news in Cartwright in 1999 was that all that was about to end. Construction of the 235-mile Trans Labrador Highway from Red Bay on Labrador's southern coast to Cartwright was due to start the following spring. When it is completed in 2003, a Newfoundland driver will be able to put his car or truck on the ferry at Flower's Cove, cross the Strait of Belle Isle to Blanc Sablon, drive the existing road to Red Bay and then roll on to Cartwright on the new one.

As a prelude, in the summer of 1999 work was well along on a 25-mile spur of the highway from Cartwright to Paradise River at the head of Sandwich Bay. The plan was to push the spur some day on through the Mealy Mountains' wilderness of rock and lakes to Goose Bay.

A revolution of sorts was at hand, and it had people in Cartwright salivating and dreaming expansive dreams. Boom times could be glimpsed coming up the new road. Woodie Lethbridge saw cheaper transportation of goods to Labrador, more tourism, more sport fishing and forestry development.

"That's the biggest money maker," he said. "We have 200-year-old timber all through the area from Paradise River to Port Hope Simpson." He cited an inventory showing that 20,000 cubic meters a year could be cut in the immediate area. But his father, Ron, a retired forest ranger, had reservations. If you cut spruce and fir and don't replant those species, he said, birch and aspen may spring up in their place. And the question arose, of course: what impact will lumbering have on Labrador's "pristine" environment that its people so often exalt. Are they ready for the scars of clear-cutting?

Blair Gillis, manager of the Northern store, saw the road bringing more business and cutting costs. He was stocking staples like sugar and flour for six months because winter ice locked out ferry deliveries. With the road connection, "we won't have to stock for more than a couple of weeks." Nor will the store have to fly in fruit from December to June, which is costly. The provincial government has been subsidizing the price of meats and perishable dairy goods in winter. The road presumably will end that.

There were cautious estimates around town of a rise in tourism. Cartwright itself holds out little in the way of tourist bait: a gift shop with some Grenfell items, the memorial to the Cartwright brothers in the cemetery and maybe a tour of the crab plant if the visitor doesn't mind getting his feet wet.

But there's more nearby. A dozen miles offshore is one of the world's great bird roosts, the Gannet Islands Ecological Reserve, home to 50,000 common murre (a black and white diver), 35,000 puffins and 8,000 other birds. A summer visitor can also sight whales and icebergs, 2,000 of which float down Iceberg Alley on the Labrador Current in a good berg year. The Wonderstrands can be visited. And of course, there is sport salmon fishing. For winter snowmobiling, packed and "groomed" trails lead out of Cartwright 130 miles down the coast. Woodie Lethbridge had no immediate plans to expand the hotel; he'll revisit the idea when the road is built.

One evening after dinner at the hotel Rod King took me in his dusty pickup out for a look at the construction of the highway spur to Paradise River. King, a husky, soft-spoken six-footer with light brown hair and mustache, is supervisor of the 25-man road crew. A native Newfoundlander, he and his blonde wife Valerie, who was with him at the hotel, now live in Goose Bay. He's been in road building for 27 years.

We drove a couple of miles to where the new road branched off, the same place where his men had gouged a quarry in a hillside. An enormous amount of rock was being used in the job, 310,000 cubic meters in the first twenty kilometers (half the projected length), King said. That works out to more than a meter and a half of rock in the roadbed which is nine and a half meters wide. The highway will ultimately be a Class A road maintained at Grade 3, which means a surface of 3/4-inch gravel allowing for heavy traffic and speeds of 70 km per hour. That would put it roughly on a par with local roads around Cartwright and several cuts above the village's streets. All are unpaved and dust machines in dry weather. The Cartwright-Paradise River project, funded 60 percent by Canada and the rest by Newfoundland, is under contract to Labrador Construction Limited, of Goose Bay.

We jounced down a mile or so of the rock-packed, tire-bruising roadbed to where the crew had constructed a small, sturdy wooden bridge over a creek. Coming our way across the bridge was a huge truck with five-foot wheels and a v-shaped body for hauling rock. Loaded, the trucks weigh 35 tons. The driver, it turned out, was Rich Martin, the younger son of Harry and Diane in Cartwright, who waved as he went by. He was earning $13.50 an hour. "Half the people working here are locals," King said, "and they're doing well." Six days a week the workday is 7 a.m. to 7 p.m. and on Sunday, in a faint nod toward the day of rest, 8 to 5.

King drove back to an existing road to show me how they get the highway across a river, in this case the Dykes River. Causeways are built out from either bank and joined by a 20-

meter Bailey Bridge, a heavily braced metal contraption that looks like something out of an Erector Set.

The road crew was commuting every day from their trailers near the hotel to the work site. Farther along, when the force gets up to forty men, King planned to set up a camp in the wilderness, with Valerie as cook. That will mean fighting black flies and mosquitoes 24 hours a day. Even at the stage of work that I saw, King called the bugs "worse than a problem"—one constant in a land of change.

Even a road partisan like King, who saw the highway bringing new prosperity, spied a dark companion coming along: "new crime." In a few years there *would* be somewhere to go with a stolen car. And in 1999 Cartwrighters already were witnessing unexpected lawbreaking.

It reminded me of a conversation I had had in 1981 with Howard "Howie" Martin, then 32, the Royal Canadian Mounted Police corporal who had been stationed in Cartwright for 15 months. A barrel-chested jogger, Martin said Cartwright was the second quietest RCMP station in Labrador (after Mary's Harbor down the coast). He had seen a few alcohol-related domestic abuse cases and two or three juvenile breaking-and-entering crimes, compared with 300 or 400 a year at his last post, Grand Bank in Newfoundland.

Why so quiet in Cartwright? "I'm not sure," he said. "They're not caught up in the rat race and society. The parents hunt and fish and trap and Skidoo. Here you don't have to have the parents drive you to the hockey rink. You get out in the woods. The kids are nice and polite. They greet you." I had noticed that, too; Trudy or Darrell Bird, encountered on the street, even with friends, would sing out a big "hi." Adults, including strangers, rarely walked by on the road without offering a "nice day."

The village had no juvenile drug problem, he said. "It wouldn't take long for someone to tell me if someone brought in drugs. Occasionally, someone may bring in some to pass around to his friends, but there is no sniffing of glue or gasoline." No comparison between Cartwright and, say, Nain up the coast, he said. "The people are different here. They all work in the summer." (The cod and salmon fisheries were still open then.) The problems surfaced in the winter, then? "Not really. You have the Lions Club meetings and dances and cutting wood and sealing. They're usually pretty tired."

Symbolic of Cartwright's placidity was Corporal Martin's role as proprietor of what passed for a zoo: a Canada goose in a chicken-wire coop in back of the station. A bulldozer, pushing dirt for the dam of the municipal water system under construction, had overturned a nest that included a week-old gosling. "You know how it is," he said with a smile, "you hand the policeman anything you don't want to deal with." He fed the fledgling corn flakes, then chicken pellets donated by someone raising chickens. The honker, now weighing ten pounds, was a major draw for the village's children who had never seen a Canada goose up close. Nonetheless, Martin was about to get rid of it; the law forbade keeping a wild creature. He would take the goose out to an island soon so it could join a flock for southward migration—a feathered Elsa.

By 1999 no Mountie was stationed in Cartwright, hadn't been for three years. They came to town briefly every couple of weeks or in an emergency. "We were told we were too good," said Gillis, the store manager, "there was too little crime here, and they had to cut the budget." The result, he said, has been an increase in petty crimes. "People drive with no registration, but they're parked when the cops are in town."

The town hardly had an American-size crime wave on its hands, but absence of the RCMP concerned many of the villagers. "It removes a deterring force," said Harry Martin, forestry and wildlife officer and a former Mountie. "If someone breaks into a store, the evidence is gone before [the RCMP] arrive, and there's no deterrence for speeders or drivers under the influence, which is a problem."

"We miss our police," said Leander "Lee" Pittman, retired principal of the Gordon Academy. Last winter a friend had had his $8,000 Skidoo stolen. It was found two months later partly dismantled. "No one was prosecuted," he said. A sizable protest followed the police budget cutback, he said, but it did no good.

As Howard Martin had observed, Cartwright's lifestyle was a factor in its peace and stability. Its winters are long, cold and snowy but the people have learned how to enjoy them. Kids play ice hockey and broomball. "On winter weekends," Diane Martin told me in 1981, "we often go off to the woods and have a boil-up. At Muddy Bay there's now a big cabin. We had a dance up there; it was lots of fun." In the spring, she said, they go to Table Bay and North River on snowmobiles and cut holes in the ice and fish for smelt when they start running. "Or we'll go all the way to Black Tickle, sixty miles, take food and gas in the komatik and put up tents to sleep in."

Movies were being shown twice a week in winter then at the Orange Lodge, vintage westerns being the most popular. And ten teams of the darts league with six men and women per team, competed once a week all winter. Wes Bird was league chief. A fellow boarder at the Birds' and I got a taste of our hosts' mastery at the dart board in their living room. The boarder and I stood Wes and Charlotte and got skunked.

The winterfest hit its peak at Easter when the town's churches held shooting matches, tug-of-wars, sales of goods and a big communal meal and dance. Cartwright's Easter Fair is a venerable tradition that has drawn people from as far away as Rigolet on Hamilton Inlet to Charlottetown a hundred miles to the south.

Winter sometimes confers its own boons. That, at least, was how the village viewed a huge influx of harp seals late in the winter of 1981. Offshore ice broke up and a big northeast storm drove the ice, laden with seals and their newborn, white-jacketed pups, five miles beyond Cartwright into Sandwich

Bay. "There were seals in the streets of Cartwright," said Les Pardy. Village septuagenarians said they had never seen the like of it.

"Six thousand pelts were taken in a week or two," said Max Mullins, federal manpower officer for the Cartwright area. "These were white harp [pup] seals—'beaters'—club 'em on the head and skin 'em. They averaged $22 a pelt. An ice breaker came in from St. John's and bought them."

Sealing is an old tradition on the coast. Grenfell himself joined a sealing ship in 1896 and counted the expedition "one of the great treats of my life." He brought in ninety-one skins for the ship. The missionary did warn that an animal producing only one pup a year could not withstand "being attacked by huge steel-protected steamers carrying hundreds of men..." The "harvest" of whitecoats by Cartwrighters, however, breached no Canadian limit, and I heard no townspeople voice the objections to sealing raised so strenuously by American conservationists.

Churches, presumably, could be counted as another stabilizing force in Cartwright life as the day of the road begins to dawn. As links with God, they are expected to be social gyrocompasses. In our conversation, Diane Martin had said that "one big change [in the community] is that so few get dressed up and go to church any more."

I didn't touch base with a church until 1991 and then it was with St. Peter's, in the east end of town, the Anglican Church of Canada parish Henry Gordon had pastored. The 7 o'clock eucharist I attended one Sunday evening seemed to bear out Diane's comment. The congregation numbered about a dozen in the well-varnished pine pews, and not very dressed up, I was happy to see; some of the members were off at summer stations.

The rector then was the Rev. James Pollard a bluff, stocky man with a brush of iron-gray hair. A former carpenter (a likely apprenticeship for a priest), he hailed from Harbor Deep in Newfoundland. He covered his 85-mile parish from Paradise River to Black Tickle by plane and a small launch surmounted by a cross on its cabin. He had used it the previous day for fishing and I asked if fishing from a cross-bearing boat improved the catch. Not that he could see, he said.

St. Peter's congregation numbered 180 but only about thirty attended regularly, he said, contributing not enough to pay for its heat and electricity, let alone his salary, which was underwritten by the Diocese of Eastern Newfoundland and Labrador.

In his sermon Sunday evening he expressed regret at sparse attendance and warned against gossip. After the service, as he gave me a lift back to the "mission" guest house in his pickup, I asked if there was any particular gossip he had in mind. No, he said, "it's always a problem in this community."

A certain level of chat in a village of six hundred people is inevitable. Everybody knows everybody, not only knows them but knows where they are, what they are doing and maybe even what they are thinking. The level of personal information can be startling. One morning I went to see a government official at his trailer office and found it empty and locked. A woman passing by on the street volunteered that he was probably getting off the Air Labrador plane that we had just seen land at the airstrip several miles away. Her hunch turned out to be perfect.

But community closeness also shows in the Labradorian's traditional impulse to help. As Hogarth Forsyth had noted, "everyone will share his last crust with his neighbor or a chance traveler." A person in trouble on broken ice finds many rescuers. People returning from a trip are not surprised to find a neighbor's home-baked loaf of bread in the fridge. A high level of kinship may contribute to this spirit. Of the 165 individuals listed in the Cartwright section of the Labrador phone book in 1991, an even hundred were grouped under eleven family names, including sixteen Dyson listings and thirteen each for Martins and Pardys. Not quite one big extended family, but getting there.

By 1999 St. Peter's had changed. Pollard had been replaced by the Rev. Jennifer Gosse, the first woman rector in Labrador history. And in her ministry the emphasis was on young people. Gosse, 27, plump and bespectacled, grew up as an only child in Mt. Pearl, twin-city of St. John's. She was only a year and a half out of seminary when we spoke in the comfortable living room of the rectory close by the church.

She was about to leave on a trip with eleven teenagers. The previous summer she had taken a dozen teens on the *Bond* to Newfoundland, spent four days touring St. John's then five days at a diocesan camp doing sports, crafts—"camp stuff." Most had never been to the island and "they loved it," she said. This summer's trip would be a reprise for a new group. The cost was $200 per youngster, paid for by diocesan committees. Tom Mugford, a parishioner, would share in the chaperoning.

She also had a project going that involved two student members of the parish cleaning up the church's historic cemetery, the one with the Cartwrights' memorial. In a blending of church and state, the province had given St. Peter's a grant to do the work.

Such activities, she hoped, would be a positive force for young people. "They see things as hopeless," she said, "Where to go, what to do? There is the fish plant, but they don't have much in the way of expectations for the future." One hopeful development was that two of the Gordon Academy's twelve graduates that year, including Dwight Lethbridge, were headed for university education. Others would go to College of the North Atlantic in Goose Bay, a community college.

Does she encounter Pollard's problem with gossip? "It produces divisions and grudge kinds of things," she said. "I preach about forgiveness, that everyone has a place in the church and about the [mistaken] idea that people from certain families are more important than people from other families."

St. Peter's is a close-knit parish, she said. "Most people in Cartwright are related to each other. Five hundred call themselves Anglicans. For many that means that if they need to be buried they want to be buried from the Anglican church." Only thirty pledge and contribute in envelopes. But winter attendance was up to forty or fifty a Sunday. At the morning service I attended one July Sunday the congregation consisted of a man and his two small kids and me. But the rector said the big service in summer is at 7 p.m. because many parishioners are working at the 7-day-a-week crab plant.

Gosse, who had been through one Cartwright winter, had promised her bishop she would weather at least one more. Finding a rector for St. Peter's is not easy. First, it's a difficult parish to cover. Every six weeks she went by plane, boat or snowmobile to Black Tickle, sixty miles away, where a tenth of the 250 people are Anglicans, and once or twice a year to the fifteen people at Paradise River. At the last service she held there, nine attended. And then there's the winter, "isolated, cold and dark," she said.

Certainly a plus, though, is that she's heard no objection to the rector being a woman. The bishop told her that wouldn't be a problem, that there had been women nurses and teachers in Labrador for a hundred years. And since Gosse broke the ice, four other Labrador parishes have acquired women priests. She can take some comfort, therefore, in being a historical figure.

16 The Grenfell

In its heyday the British Empire grew on a rich diet of mercantile interests. Tea, tobacco, fish, ivory, sugar, spices—commodities like these nourished the realm. With their extraction, though, came exploitation, and nowhere was that truer than in Newfoundland, the empire's founding block. A shipmate of Humphrey Gilbert wrote home in 1583, "There are inexhaustible supplies of fish, so that those who travel here do good business." Did they ever. The controlling ethic in the colony's early years was maximum return from the teeming cod banks for England's West Country merchants, owners of the fishing fleet.

"The British Government had no intention of seeing the ship fishery die or be swallowed up by a growing and aggressive local fishery," historian Frederick W. Rowe wrote. "Apparently the government had given up any hope of destroying the permanent communities, but it did not want Newfoundland to become a costly and vexatious colonial experiment like New England, a thorn in the flesh of the Mother Country."

Thus, settlement on the island was discouraged and local power placed in the hands of the fishing admirals. Britain's 1699 Act to Encourage Trade to Newfoundland gave the admirals the right to settle disputes between fishing ship masters and settlers. One can guess how many decisions went to the settlers. The sole appeal was to the commander of any British warship that might be in port.

With that as a colonial heritage, it is easier to understand the profit-centered climate of neglect that Grenfell and his comrades encountered when they arrived at the island's northern peninsula and Labrador in 1892. As England had treated its colony, so Newfoundland was using the peninsula. Labrador was even farther out in the cold.

Against daunting odds, on shoestring budgets and with heroic effort, Grenfell and his mission set out to fill the vacuum, to bring essential services to the people—beginning with medical care, then schools, orphanages, supplementary employment, a better diet, boat building: what a caring government might provide or foster. In health care they succeeded to the point that some in the St. John's medical community were grumbling about what they perceived to be an inordinately high quality of service in St. Anthony.

The WOP system was phased out in the mid-1970s, followed in 1981 by the demise of the mission itself. But, to a surprising degree, the spirit lives on: "The Grenfell," Peter Roberts calls it. "The Grenfell obsession is not as unusual as the uninitiated might suspect," he has written. "Many people had it in the past. Many still do. There is something about this work, the people, the place, that gets a hold on you and it does not let go easily... I know many, many people who count 'the Grenfell' as the major feature of their lives."

The Grenfell is alive and functioning in the United States in two organizations, the Grenfell Association of America, in New York, and the New England Grenfell Association in Boston. The GAA, founded in 1907, is much the larger of the two, with about $20 million in assets and $1 million a year in disposable income; the NEGA's $10.5 million produces an annual $520,000. Both hold annual dinner or lunch meetings, free for those interested.

Just about all of the two incomes go to continue Grenfell's work of helping people up on the coast. Grants are funneled through the International Grenfell Association (IGA) in St. John's which has final say on who gets what. The GAA is guided by a statement that its mission "is to improve medical and dental services, public health services, educational opportunities and the overall quality of life in the Grenfell area following the example set by Sir Wilfred T. Grenfell."

To some extent outlays are governed by specific terms of gifts bestowed over the years. A significant part of the GAA funds, for example, (I couldn't find anyone who knew the exact amount) came from a pretty woman named Louie Alice Hall who died in Rochester, N.Y., in 1944. Louie Hall's brother, Charles Martin Hall in 1886 discovered the process of cheaply and commercially producing aluminum: electrolysis of purified alumina dissolved in molten cryolite. Charles Hall was a chemistry student at Oberlin College when he began his experiments. He continued using the college laboratory after graduation in 1885 and eight months later broke through with the discovery (French metallurgist Paul Heroult reached the identical finding independently at about the same time). Hall enlisted the support of the Mellon family in founding the Pittsburgh Reduction Company which metamorphosed into the Aluminum Company of America (Alcoa). As Alcoa's vice president, he became a wealthy man and through him Louie Hall came to own thousands of shares of Alcoa stock. She became a devoted supporter of Grenfell and his mission. In her will she gave the Grenfell Association of America 1,000 shares of Alcoa stock plus her residuary estate, specifying that it should benefit the hospital at St. Anthony. It still does.

The grants from the two American Grenfell organizations and from the Grenfell Association of Great Britain and Ireland (GAGBI), as they flow through the IGA, are much appreciated on the coast. "The IGA grants are very critical for our operations," says John Budgell, executive director of Grenfell Regional Health Services. "We use them for equipment and research. Sometimes that's the only money for research." The service also launches new programs with IGA money. Example: an occupational therapist for the elderly in the John Gray facility. "Then we used that experience to demonstrate [to the government] the need for and value of such work."

The funds go far beyond medical care and rehabilitation, however, to include reading programs, playgrounds, computer software, summer camps and intern programs. The NEGA gives half a dozen scholarships a year to coast students pursuing medical or teaching degrees. In a March 2000 editorial, the St. Anthony newspaper, *Northern Pen*, thanked the IGA and its allied associations for having been wise stewards of their investments and for their "interest in the affairs of the region and for their dedication in preserving such an important program. It's one of the true lasting legacies to the benevolence of Dr. Grenfell and his followers."

The grants may be appreciated but they are not beyond controversy. The GRHS board has told the International Grenfell Association that it should give up its "custodial and charitable role and let the people of the coast assume responsibility for their destiny." Any attempt to transfer funds from the American organizations to GRHS, however, would entail lengthy and expensive litigation and wouldn't be worth it, said Cecil Ashdown, a long-time GAA board member. Moreover, the IGA has not cut itself off from the coast; on its board are two Newfoundlanders and two Labradorians.

The Grenfell is not just an institutional matter. As Roberts said, it lives on in people's hearts, mostly those of former volunteers. There were reasons enough, however, to disband the WOP system in the '70s. For one, breadwinners on the coast did not cotton to volunteers doing work that they could have been paid for, especially as unemployment rose in the province. And second, the WOPs themselves had started changing in the upheaving 1960s.

Roberts began his Grenfell experience as a medical volunteer in 1971 but knew of the mission well before that. The volunteer of the 1930s and '40s "was a different kind of person than in the '60s and '70s," he said. "[Formerly] when a volunteer was told to shovel coal, he did it, and that was that and he didn't say boo." WOPs of later times, he said, "sometimes came with a lot of excess baggage. I'd find a volunteer sitting on the wharf playing a banjo. If you had a hundred volunteers you were guaranteed to find ten or fifteen who had something going on that interfered with their ability to contribute effectively. It came to baby sitting and it wasn't worth the effort."

Adolescents, of course, are an unsettled lot. "Some were as straight as could be, A-plus in all ways," he said, "and some weren't. We did not have the ability to look after them. When the Peace Corps developed, it took many of those people. It did what we were doing but in a fully organized way, did it in a better way." Dr. Gordon Thomas, Roberts's predecessor as executive director of the mission, had this take on the subject: "The volunteer program helped the volunteers more than it helped the people on the coast."

No question, the volunteers benefited. Yet testimony of the likes of Grenfell himself and Tony Paddon on the contributions of volunteers still stands. People like Pumphrey and his gang did valuable work, and they continue to carry the Grenfell torch like Olympians running to ignite the flame.

What is it? "For me the spirit which Grenfell disseminated and which remained within the organization for so many years after his death," Dr. John M. Gray, medical chief at St. Anthony, told the 1980 GAA dinner, "was something that makes for the best in society. His desire to see justice and show compassion, his upholding of truth and honesty—these are attributes which I believe make for a stable and happy society where men and women are guided by their consciences rather than by the clock or their pocket."

It is the spirit which prompted the IGA in 1981 to transfer millions of dollars' worth of facilities to Grenfell Regional Health Services, the provincial agency, for one dollar bill, now framed and on a wall in Curtis Hospital, and later to give free and clear 875 acres of mission ground to "the crown"—the government—including 175 acres in Cartwright.

If anyone on the two continents exemplifies The Grenfell, though, it is Bevan Pumphrey, head WOP of the great pipeline dig at Cartwright and one of the last survivors among Grenfell's personal friends. When Sibby and I were in England in March 2000 we had lunch with him and his wife,

Jacqueline, in Canterbury not far from their home in Tenterden, Kent. Then 87 and with failing eyesight, he was vigorous and full of his usual good humor and stories. (Despite my strenuous efforts, he grabbed and paid the check in the small Italian restaurant we had chosen.)

He was saddened that the Grenfell Association of Great Britain and Ireland, of which he was once executive committee chairman, was going out of business. But "on a happier note," he had written in a letter, "I have been given the honour and privilege of principal speaker at the final annual general meeting [of GAGBI] at the Royal Overseas League in London on 13 May to recount my experiences during my visits to Newfoundland and Labrador in 1931 and 1987 and my times with Wilfred Grenfell on the Coast and in England..."

At the May session he might have considered repeating the story he told at the 1990 GAGBI meeting, to the effect that great people can get away with almost anything. Grenfell, he said, was proof of this. Giving a prestigious lecture in London before the Duke and Duchess of York (later King George VI and Queen Elizabeth), he was supposed to talk about his mission. Instead, he launched into a discussion of China. Three times the meeting's chairman sent him notes and three times Grenfell looked at them and threw them on the floor. "At the close," said Pumphrey, "he was rapturously applauded and no one seemed the least annoyed that he had given the wrong talk."

At the final GAGBI meeting Pumphrey did indeed recount his Labrador adventures and encounters with Grenfell. This time it was the right talk. And, as with his famous mentor, he was rapturously applauded.

Bibliography

Myron Arms, *Riddle of the Ice*, Anchor Books, Doubleday, New York, 1998.

Audubon and His Journals, Vol. 1, Chelsea House, New York, 1983.

A. Scott Berg, *Lindbergh*, G. P. Putnam's Sons, New York, 1998

Winston Churchill, *The Grand Alliance*, Houghton Mifflin Co., Boston, 1974

Henry Gordon, *Labrador Parson, An Account of Life in the Labrador, 1915-1925*, unpublished, Memorial University of Newfoundland Library, St. John's.

Wilfred T. Grenfell:
Adrift on an Ice Pan, Houghton Mifflin Co., Boston, 1909.
A Labrador Doctor, Houghton Mifflin, Boston, 1919.
What Christ Means to Me, Houghton Mifflin, New York, 1927.
Forty Years for Labrador, Houghton Mifflin, Boston, 1932.
The Romance of Labrador, The Macmillan Co., New York, 1934.
Grenfell Historical Society papers, St. Anthony, Newfoundland.

Harold Horwood, *Newfoundland*, Macmillan of Canada, Toronto, 1977

Douglas How, *Night of the Caribou*, Lancelot Press, Hantsport, Nova Scotia, 1988.

Helge Ingstad, *Vinland Ruins Prove Vikings Found the New World*, National Geographic Magazine, November 1964.

J. Lennox Kerr, *Wilfred Grenfell, His Life and Work*, Dodd, Mead & Co., New York, 1959.

Sally Lou LeMessurier, *The Fishery of Newfoundland and Labrador*, Memorial University of Newfoundland, St. John's, 1980.

Anne Morrow Lindbergh, *Locked Rooms and Open Doors*, Harcourt Brace Jovanovich, Inc., New York, 1974.

Elliott Merrick, *True North*, University of Nebraska Press., Lincoln, 1989.

William J. Miller, *Henry Cabot Lodge*, James H. Heineman Inc., New York, 1967.

Samuel Eliot Morison, *The European Discovery of America - The Northern Voyages*, Oxford University Press, New York, 1971.

Joe Alex Morris, *Nelson Rockefeller, a Biography*, Harper & Brothers, New York, 1960.

Peter Neary and Patrick O'Flaherty, editors, *By Great Waters, a Newfoundland and Labrador Anthology*, University of Toronto Press, Toronto, 1974.

W. A. Paddon, *Labrador Doctor, My Life with the Grenfell Mission*, James Lorimer & Co., Toronto, 1989.

Bevan Pumphrey, *Through the Years*, Intype, London, 1994.

Ronald Rompkey:
 Grenfell of Labrador - A Biography, University of Toronto Press, Toronto, 1991.
 Labrador Odyssey - The Journal and Photographs of Eliot Curwen on the Second Voyage of Wilfred Grenfell, 1893, McGill-Queen's University Press, Montreal, 1996.

Frederick W. Rowe, *A History of Newfoundland and Labrador*, McGraw-Hill Ryerson Ltd., Toronto, 1980.

Ted Russell, *The Chronicles of Uncle Mose - Smokeroom on the Kyle*, St. John's.

Francis B. Sayre, *Glad Adventure*, Macmillan Co., New York, 1957.

John Steffler, *The Afterlife of George Cartwright*, Henry Holt & Co., New York, 1992.

Robert Stewart, *Labrador -The World's Wild Places*, Time-Life Books, Amsterdam, 1977.

Them Days, Happy Valley-Goose Bay, Labrador, 1984.
Gordon W. Thomas, *From Sled to Satellite*, Irwin Publishing Inc., 1987.
TIME Capsule - 1941, Time Inc., New York, 1941.
Milton Viorst, editor, *Making a Difference - The Peace Corps at 25*, Weidenfeld & Nicolson, New York, 1986.
Vox MeDal, *The Voice of Medical Alumni of Dalhousie University*, Fall, 1988.
Yale University Library, *Wilfred T. Grenfell Papers, Manuscripts and Archives*.

ndex

AINSCOW, Donald 126-127
ANDERSON, Bill 121
ANDREWS, George 20
ANDREWS, Joseph 72
ANNE, Princess 173-175
ARMS, Myron 171
ARMSTRONG, Mrs Harvey 67
ARNOLD, Benedict 53
ASHALL, Clara 154-155
ASHDOWN, Cecil 196
ASHER, William Max 56
ATTUIOCK, 53
AUDUBON, John James 150
AUSTEN, Kate 83
BADGER, Theodore 29
BALBO, Italo 179-181
BALDWIN, Hanson W 70
BARTLETT, Bob 22
BEAVERBROOK, Lord 61
BENSON, Harriet 93-94
BINZEN, Peter 115
BIRD, Charlie 3 7-8 55-56 62
BIRD, Charlotte 47 158-160 169 182 188
BIRD, Darrell 158-159 186
BIRD, Harvey 3 8 56 63
BIRD, Mickey 56
BIRD, Roly 152-153
BIRD, Sharon 158
BIRD, Trudy 158-159 186
BIRD, Wesley 158-159 188

BIRDSEYE, Clarence 2 167
BIRDSEYE, Eleanor 167-168
BIRDSEYE, Kellogg 168
BLAKE, Ira 87-88
BOB, Beamon 116
BONET, Jordi 174
BOUVIER, Jacqueline 84
BOWDRING, Ed 135-136
BREIDEN, Nancy 120
BROMLEY, Bernard 124 174
BROWN, William O 63
BRYAN, Robert A 71
BUDGELL, John 195
BURDETT, Gladys 144 Joshua 169
BURNHAM, Anne Hopkins 83-87
BURNHAM, Bradford 86
BYRD, Richard E 15
CABOT, John 33 137
CAMPBELL, John 90
CARTER, Jimmy 89 105
CARTIER, Jacques 37
CARTWRIGHT, George 4 51-54 63-64 170 177-178 184
CARTWRIGHT, John 54
CAUBVICK, 53
CHURCHILL, Winston 35-36 61

CLARK, Denley 48
CLARK, Scoville 77
COLGATE, Josephine 93-94
COMPTON, Hazel 57
CRENSHAW, John 38 63 108
CROFT, Jenny 124 133
CURL, Austin 133-135 137-138
CURL, Solomon 134 137-138
CURTIS, Charles S 49 67 75 95-96
DAUBENY, Joseph 53
DAVIES, Marion 59
DAWE, Levi 19-20
DECKER, George 128
DELANO, William A 70
DIACK, Leslie 84-85
DIMAGGIO, Joe 29
DITZEN, Stuart 114
DUMAS, Renee 106
DYSON, Charley 85-86
DYSON, Charlotte 160
DYSON, Esau 86
ELSON, Bill 160
EMERSON, Faye 59
ERICSSON, Leif 128-129 137 161
FERNANDEZ, Joao 37
FORD, Henry 56 93
FORSYTH, C Hogarth 7 40-41 44 46-49 54 57-58 61 64-65 85-87 104 108 148-149 190

FORSYTH, Clayre Ruland 41 46
FRANKFURTER, Felix 79
FUDGE, Hugh 136
GANNETT, Eleanor 167
GILBERT, Humphrey 115-116 193
GILLIS, Blair 171 184
GORDON, Delrose 132-133
GORDON, Henry 22 51 54-55 152-155 157 189 191
GOSSE, Jennifer 191-192
GRAHAM, Billy 22
GRAY, John M 125 195 197
GRENFELL, Anne 94 122
GRENFELL, Pascoe 5
GRENFELL, Wilfred T 1-3 5-7 9-17 19-25 27-29 36-41 46-47 49 53 56-57 59 61-65 67 69-74 76-80 83-84 86 88-94 96-99 103-105 111 113 116-118 122-124 126 129 130-131 133 137-143 146 152 155 161 167 174 178-179 181 184 189 193-198
GRIMES, John 53 177-178
HALL, Charles 195
HALL, Louie Alice 195
HANCOCK, Charlie 15 20
HANCOCK, James 16
HAYDEN, Buddy 114
HEARST, William Randolph 59
HERIULFSON, Biarni 37
HERMAN, Gene 114

HEROULT, Paul 195
HISCOCK, Eugene 143 178
HITLER, Adolf 35-36 179
HOWE, Alison 142 149-150
INGSTAD, Helge 128
JARDINE, Marjory 67-69
JOHNSON, Samuel 55 163
KEDDIE, Kate M 62
KENNEDY, John F 27
KING, Claudia 104
KING, Harry 30 36 55-57 64 99-104 106 109 185-186
KING, John 99 103-104
KING, Mary 103
KING, Rod 185-186
KING, Valerie 185-186
KUSHELOFF, Dave 114
LEARNING, Sam 153
   Will 153
LEMAY, Curtis 63
LERCH, Thomas 7
LETHBRIDGE, Alice 162
LETHBRIDGE, Chesley 48 163
LETHBRIDGE, Dwight 167
LETHBRIDGE, Garland 167
LETHBRIDGE, Perry 164
LETHBRIDGE, Ronald 162-165
LETHBRIDGE, Ronald Jr 166
LETHBRIDGE, Woodrow 161-162 166 183-184
LINDBERGH, Anne 180-181
LINDBERGH, Charles A 180-181
LINDBERGH, Charles Jr 181
LODGE, Henry Cabot 2 96-97
LOREN, Sophia 106
LOWELL, Eleanor 98
LOWELL, John 97-98
LOWELL, Ralph 97
LUTHER, Jessie 132
MACARTHUR, Douglas 79-80
MACDONALD, Angus 31
MARK, Sam 133
MARTIN, Diane 147-148 157 185 188-189
MARTIN, Harry 147 185 187
MARTIN, Howard 186 188
MARTIN, Rich 147 185
MAYNARD, Edwin 73
MCGEE, Robina 95
MCLEAN, Malcolm 43
   Murdoch 87
MCNEILL, Samuel Edgar 2 3 6 20
MERRICK, Elliott 80-83 87-88 91
MERRILL, Edwin 96
MICHELIN, Robert 60
MONTAGU, John 51
MOODY, Dwight L 22
MOORES, William 178
MORROW, Dwight 181
MUGFORD, Tom 191

MULLINS, Max 169 189
MULLINS, Shirley 169
MUNDEN, Clark 71
MUSSOLINI, Benito 179
PADDON, Harry 3 34 41 73 80-83 118 154
PADDON, Mina 34
PADDON, Richard 34 43
PADDON, William Anthony 71 83-84 86-87 116 140 155 197
PALMER, Douglas 77
PARDY, Leslie 171-172 189
PARDY, Malcolm 182
PARSONS, Hayward 153
PASTEUR, Louis 21
PEARY, Robert 13 22 78
PHILIP, Prince 63
PIKE, James A 102
PITTMAN, Leander 188
POLLARD, James 189 191
POOLE, Lydia 139
PRESCOTT, Kitty 133
PUMPHREY, Bevan 3-7 14 63 69 74 139 159 197-198
PUTNAM, David 104
PUTNAM, Nancy 103
QUEZON, Manuel 79
REAGAN, Ronald 113
REID, George 19-20
REID, Levi 19-20
REID, William 20
RICHARDS, Henry 48
RILEY, D L 13
RING, Jim 116
ROBBINS, Oliver W 3

ROBERTS, Edward 123
ROBERTS, Harry 123
ROBERTS, Peter J 123-127 140 142 155 174 194 196-197
ROCKEFELLER, David 92
ROCKEFELLER, John D Jr 74 91
ROCKEFELLER, Laurance 2 39-40 91-92
ROCKEFELLER, Nelson 2 39-40 91-93
ROMPKEY, Ronald G 71 99
ROOSEVELT, Elliott 58-60 181
ROOSEVELT, Franklin 12 29 61 79 180
ROOSEVELT, Theodore 12 79 178
ROWE, Frederick W 193
RUPRECHT, Archibald L 14 30 32 38 55 57 64 103 107-111
RUPRECHT, David 110
RUPRECHT, Nancy 109
RUPRECHT, Wendy 110
SALTER, Robert B 49 95-96
SARSFIELD, Irene 140 155
SARSFIELD, Peter 139-146 148-150 155
SAYRE, Elizabeth 79
SAYRE, Francis B 77-80
SAYRE, Jessie 79
SCHWEITZER, Albert 11-12
SCRANTON, William 61
SELBY, Mrs 52-53

SHEPPARD, Albert 131
SHRIVER, Sargent 27
SILK, George 83
SIMMS, Alec 67
SIMMS, Reuben 15
SIMONDS, Lisa 73
SLIMON, Jean 146-147 150-151
SMITH, Shirley Soule 89-91
SPALDING, Katie 47-48 57
STEELE, Jack 94
STUDD, C T 22
STUDD, J E 22
SUBRAMANIAM, Leela 161
SWIFT, Charles 105
SWIFT, George 30 34 37-38 40 55 57-58 61-63 65 105-107 146
SWIFT, Renée 106-107
TAVERNER, Benjamin 31
TAVERNER, Harold 31
TAVERNER, Stanley 31
THEROUX, Paul 27
THIBAULT, The Rev 68
THOMAS, Gordon W 49 71 117 123 125 128 146 197

TOLAND, Sibby 197
VANCE, Cyrus R 87-89
WAGSTAFF, Cornelia
 Scranton 61-63 65-66
 Samuel 65 105
WAKEFIELD, W B 2 71
WATTS, Jack 8
WESCOTT, Eleanor
 Cushman 72 74-75 92
WETHERILL, William 81-82
WHYTE, William H Jr 92
WIGGINS, Gordon 157 182
WILKE, A W 31
WILLETT, Capt 80-81
WILLIAMS, George 64 77-78 157
 Liz 154
 Stewart 8
 Ted 29
WINSLOW, Jackie 30 38
WOLCOTT, "Grandpa" 34
WYGANT, Henry S Jr 101
YU-HSIANG, Feng 97
ZWICKY, Steve 120

Harry G. Toland

Harry Toland spent the summer of his freshman year at Yale doing manual labor at the Grenfell medical mission station in Cartwright, Labrador. After finishing college he spent three years in the Marine Corps in World War II and then began a 42-year career in journalism. More than 31 of those yeas were spent at *The Evening Bulletin* in Philadelphia as labor reporter, regional columnist, deputy metropolitan editor and editorial writer/columnist. Before retirement he was for two years associate editor of *The Episcopalian*, then the Episcopal Church's national journal.

Toland returned to Newfoundland and Labrador three times in recent years gathering material for *A Sort of Peace Corps*. The author of two other books, he lives in Wallingford, Pa., with his wife Sibby.

www.ingramcontent.com/pod-product-compliance
Lightning Source LLC
Chambersburg PA
CBHW070736160426
43192CB00009B/1463